M000189931

Scripture Confessions

Confessions

— COLLECTION —

Scripture
Confessions

— COLLECTION —

LIFE-CHANGING WORDS
OF FAITH FOR EVERY DAY

Keith & Megan Provance

CONTENTS

INTRODUCTION

This powerful book is a unique compilation of Scriptures that will enable you to declare the Word of God over your life for victorious living, healing, prosperity, and the situations you face on a daily basis.

God's Word makes it perfectly clear that it is God's will for you to have a victorious, healthy, and prosperous life. These are God's promises to you. But just because this is God's will for your life doesn't mean it will automatically happen. You have to believe His promises, reach out for them in faith, and snatch them for yourself. Everything you receive from God, you receive by faith. A key factor in releasing your faith is the words that come out of your mouth. There is power released into your life when you speak God's Word. It is a vital part of appropriating God's promises and activating spiritual forces that will bring God's promises to manifestation.

Jesus said in Mark 11:23-24 that *"whosoever shall say unto this mountain, Be thou removed, and be thou cast into the sea; and shall not doubt in his heart, but shall believe that those things which he saith shall come to pass; he shall have whatsoever he saith. Therefore I say unto you, What things soever ye desire, when ye pray, believe that ye receive them, and ye shall have them."*

Speak to the mountain in your life and it will obey you! Wow! Isn't that awesome?

The confessions in this book are faith declarations based on God's Word. We encourage you to speak them daily over your life. No matter what you are going through, there is hope, there is help and there is life-altering power in speaking God's Word. Be faithful to speak His Word. Release your faith as you speak, and say these declarations boldly. Speak with power and authority. Release your faith and lay claim to the promises that are rightfully yours. Now, start speaking—and get ready to experience the release of God's power in your life!

SCRIPTURE CONFESSIONS FOR VICTORIOUS LIVING

GOD IS THE FIRST THING ON MY MIND

Today is truly going to be a good day. This is the day my God has created and I will rejoice and be glad in it. I am in stride and in rhythm with God's good, pleasing, and perfect will for my life. I will love the Lord my God with all of my heart, with all of my soul, and with all of my strength. I am a child of God. God is for me, God is with me, and God is in me. I am prepared to take on anything and everything because greater is He that is in me than he that is in the world.

May God direct my steps today. I am healed, healthy, and whole. No matter what happens today, I know my God will be there to see me through. Today, I choose to let God's love, God's life, and God's light shine through me.

Blessings of provision, health, and favor are mine. I am not easily distracted but focused, disciplined, and committed to God's plans for my life. I am confident and courageous. I can do all things through Christ who strengthens me. He is my strength, my help, and my life.

Scripture Confessions

This is the day which the LORD hath made; we will rejoice and be glad in it.

PSALM 118:24

But he was wounded for our transgressions, he was bruised for our iniquities: the chastisement of our peace was upon him; and with his stripes we are healed.

ISAIAH 53:5

Be strong in the Lord, and in the power of his might.

EPHESIANS 6:10

Christ hath redeemed us from the curse of the law, being made a curse for us: for it is written, Cursed is every one that hangeth on a tree.

GALATIANS 3:13

Love the LORD your God with all your heart and with all your soul and with all your strength. These commandments that I give you today are to be upon your hearts.

DEUTERONOMY 6:5-6 NIV

THE GREATER ONE IN ME

Greater is He that is in me, than he that is in the world. The Holy Spirit in me is greater than Satan and all the forces of darkness. God in me is greater than sin, sickness, and disease. God in me is greater than lack, want, and need. God in me is greater than any circumstance I might face, greater than any obstacle that comes up before me.

God in me is greater than any challenge that comes into my life. God in me is greater than any adversity that comes against me. He is greater than my own doubts, insecurities, or uncertainties. He is greater than anything this life can throw at me.

The same Spirit that raised Christ Jesus from the dead lives in me; He quickens and makes alive my mortal body. It's not my talent, my wisdom, or my strength but by His Spirit that I succeed in life.

I am more than a conqueror through Jesus Christ. I can face the circumstances of life with boldness and confidence. He puts me over; He causes me to succeed. The Greater One lives in me; I cannot fail!

Scripture Confessions

Ye are of God, little children, and have overcome them: because greater is he that is in you, than he that is in the world.

1 JOHN 4:4

These things I have spoken unto you, that in me ye might have peace. In the world ye shall have tribulation: but be of good cheer; I have overcome the world.

JOHN 16:33

Nay, in all these things we are more than conquerors through him that loved us.

ROMANS 8:37

But if the Spirit of him that raised up Jesus from the dead dwell in you, he that raised up Christ from the dead shall also quicken your mortal bodies by his Spirit that dwelleth in you.

ROMANS 8:11

I AM A WORLD OVERCOMER

I am a world overcomer, strong in the Lord and the power of His might. I am born of God and that makes me a world overcomer. I am confident, courageous, and undaunted in my faith, even when I experience tribulation, tests, and trials. I will not succumb to distress, frustration, or defeat. I have been designed by God to succeed in this life. Through God and the authority He has given to me, I can overcome any obstacle or challenge I might face. I can overcome even during tough economic times. I can overcome even when the odds are against me. I can overcome unexpected, unforeseen setbacks—no matter how I feel, no matter what my present circumstances, regardless of the failures of the past, regardless of what happens around me—I shall overcome! I will never give up, I will never surrender, and I will fight until I win. The battle is the Lord's and the victory is mine. I am a world overcomer!

Scripture Confessions

Every God-begotten person conquers the world's ways. The conquering power that brings the world to its knees is our faith. The person who wins out over the world's ways is simply the one who believes Jesus is the Son of God.

1 JOHN 5:4-5 MSG

But thanks be to God, Who in Christ always leads us in triumph [as trophies of Christ's victory] and through us spreads and makes evident the fragrance of the knowledge of God everywhere.

2 CORINTHIANS 2:14 AMP

We are of God, little children, and have overcome them: because greater is he that is in you, than he that is in the world.

1 JOHN 4:4

I can do all things through Christ which strengtheneth me.

PHILIPPIANS 4:13

BECOMING THE PERSON GOD SAYS I AM

Ichoose to live a godly life before my family and friends. I am disciplined concerning the priorities of my life. I manage my time in an effective and efficient manner. I am sensitive to the needs of my family and friends. I have God's wisdom and discernment concerning all my decisions.

I am loving, caring, and compassionate toward others. I keep my cool during times of stress and do not become frustrated and lose my temper. If I do something that is wrong or offensive, I am quick to repent. Because I live a Spirit-controlled life, I am peaceful, consistent, and faithful. I walk in love at all times, and I am quick to provide encouragement and inspiration to those who need it.

I know the voice of the Holy Spirit, and I am quick to obey His voice. God's presence and peace adorn my life like a beautiful robe. God's grace and favor are a crown upon my head. His goodness and mercy follow me all the days of my life.

Scripture Confessions

...we should live soberly, righteously, and godly, in this present world.

TITUS 2:12

If any of you lack wisdom, let him ask of God, that giveth to all men liberally, and upbraideth not; and it shall be given him.

JAMES 1:5

...be thou an example of the believers, in word, in conversation, in charity, in spirit, in faith, in purity.

1 TIMOTHY 4:12

RENEWING MY MIND

I dedicate myself to renewing my mind by reading, meditating, and speaking God's Word. It is my desire to keep my mind pure and clear from anything that would hurt or weaken me spiritually. I think on things that are pure, lovely, just, of a good report, virtuous, and praiseworthy.

I choose to think about good things, and I refuse thoughts that are inappropriate. I cast down vain imaginations. I will not let doubt, worry, or fear pollute my mind. I will be quick to respond to wrong thoughts and desires by replacing them with proper thoughts and by speaking God's Word over my life.

I refuse to fill my mind with the poison of gossip, backbiting, and jealousy. I will guard and protect my mind by not watching, reading, or listening to anything that is not pleasing to the Lord. I make a quality decision to meditate on God's Word and to keep my mind pure and undefiled, that I might be receptive to God's voice and ever ready to do His will.

I consecrate my mind, my will, and my emotions to God for His service.

Scripture Confessions

And be not conformed to this world: but be ye transformed by the renewing of your mind, that ye may prove what is that good, and acceptable, and perfect, will of God.

ROMANS 12:2

Finally, brethren, whatsoever things are true, whatsoever things are honest, whatsoever things are just, whatsoever things are pure, whatsoever things are lovely, whatsoever things are of good report; if there be any virtue, and if there be any praise, think on these things.

PHILIPPIANS 4:8

Casting down imaginations, and every high thing that exalteth itself against the knowledge of God, and bringing into captivity every thought to the obedience of Christ.

2 CORINTHIANS 10:5

WISDOM

God's wisdom flowing in me provides guidance, insight, and discernment in every area of my life.

God's wisdom in me gives me foresight and understanding concerning all issues that come before me. His wisdom teaches me how to properly manage my time and prioritize my activities; therefore, I am effective and efficient in all I do.

God's wisdom helps me succeed in every area of my life. My job and business flourish because His wisdom operates in my life. I am able to make significant and meaningful contributions to the lives of my family, friends, and business associates because of that wisdom. I am not fooled or deceived by others because God's wisdom protects me from deceivers and liars and the snares of the enemy. My steps are ordered and directed of God.

God's wisdom in me keeps me from making poor choices. I am an excellent decision-maker because I operate with prudence and discretion. When faced with many possible choices, God's wisdom gives me peace in my heart that I might recognize what are the right decisions that I need to make. I have the mind of Christ. I operate and conduct my life with His wisdom.

Scripture Confessions

If any of you lack wisdom, let him ask of God, that giveth to all men liberally, and upbraideth not; and it shall be given him.

JAMES 1:5

The steps of a good man are ordered by the LORD: and he delighteth in his way.

PSALM 37:23

Through wisdom is an house builded; and by understanding it is established.

PROVERBS 24:3

FAVOR

I am blessed and highly favored with God and with man. The favor of God is operating and functioning in my life. It surrounds my life as a shield. His favor goes before me and prepares my way. Favor opens doors of blessing and opportunity in my life. Wherever I go and whatever I do, God's favor is with me and on me. God's favor is operating and functioning in every area of my life. I have favor with my family, on my job, and in all of my relationships. All my endeavors are blessed. God's blessings of favor come to me every day. Whatever I set my hand to prospers and succeeds because of His favor. God's favor brings promotion and increase to my life. God's favor fills my life with overflowing blessing, peace, joy, fulfillment, and abundance. God's favor takes me where my own ability and wisdom cannot. Wonderful things are always happening to me, so it's a surety that something good is going to happen to me today.

Scripture Confessions

A good man obtaineth favour of the Lord; but a man of wicked devises will he condemn.

PROVERBS 12:2

When a man's ways please the LORD, he maketh even his enemies to be at peace with him.

PROVERBS 16:7

For thou, LORD, wilt bless the righteous; with favour wilt thou compass him as with a shield.

PSALM 5:12

I know thy works: behold, I have set before thee an open door, and no man can shut it....

REVELATION 3:8

WALKING IN LOVE

Because God's love is in me, I declare that I endure long, I am patient, and I am kind. I am never envious and never boil over with jealousy. I am not boastful or vain, and I do not display myself haughtily. I am not rude and unmannerly, and I do not act unbecomingly. I do not insist on my own rights or my own way; I am not self-seeking, touchy, fretful, or resentful. I take no account of an evil done to me; I pay no attention to a suffered wrong. I do not rejoice at injustice and unrighteousness, but I rejoice when right and truth prevail. I bear up under anything and everything that comes. I am ever ready to believe the best of others. My hopes are fadeless under all circumstances. I endure everything without weakening because God's love in me never fails.

God's love in me reaches out to people around me. God's love in me ministers hope, peace, and encouragement to others. God's love in me is a testimony of His grace, mercy, and joy to everyone around me. The love of God is the guiding force of my life.

Scripture Confessions

This is my commandment, That ye love one another, as I have loved you.

JOHN 15:12

Charity suffereth long, and is kind; charity envieth not; charity vaunteth not itself, is not puffed up, doth not behave itself unseemly, seeketh not her own, is not easily provoked, thinketh no evil; rejoiceth not in iniquity, but rejoiceth in the truth; beareth all things, believeth all things, hopeth all things, endureth all things. Charity never faileth.

1 CORINTHIANS 13:4-8

No man hath seen God at any time. If we love one another, God dwelleth in us, and his love is perfected in us.

1 JOHN 4:12

STAND AGAINST SATAN

Satan is a defeated foe and he has no power over me. Jesus Christ, my Lord and Savior, defeated Satan; Jesus spoiled principalities, demonic powers, and made a show of them openly. Satan is under my feet; Jesus has given me authority over Satan and all the powers of darkness. I give the devil no place in my life. I am not afraid of the devil—he's afraid of me!

No weapon formed against me shall prosper. Though the enemy comes in like a flood, the Lord shall raise up a standard against him. In the name of Jesus and by the power of His blood, I come against any curse or evil assignment that Satan has arrayed against me. I break the power of Satan and the forces of darkness aligned against me; I render them null and void of any power to hurt or harm me.

I stand strong in my faith against the strategies of the devil. Greater is He that is in me than He that is in the world— greater than sickness, disease, poverty, and lack; greater than all the forces of darkness. I will not be deceived, snared, or caught off guard by demonic influences. I overcome evil with good— with prayer, God's Word, and the armor of God. I win every battle against Satan and the forces of darkness.

Scripture Confessions

For we wrestle not against flesh and blood, but against principalities, against powers, against the rulers of the darkness of this world, against spiritual wickedness in high places.

EPHESIANS 6:12

Wherefore take unto you the whole armour of God, that ye may be able to withstand in the evil day, and having done all, to stand.

EPHESIANS 6:13

Ye are of God, little children, and have overcome them: because greater is he that is in you, than he that is in the world.

1 JOHN 4:4

FREEDOM FROM FEAR

I will not allow fear to torment, influence, or control my life. I give no place to fear. I will not give in to the temptation to be afraid. I am not worried or filled with anxiety. I do not fear the future. Though I may walk through the valley of the shadow of death, I will fear no evil, for God's rod and staff comfort me.

I am not afraid of bad news because God is my rock, my fortress, and my deliverer. God gives me the strength and courage to handle any situation. God has promised that He will never leave me or forsake me. God has delivered me from fear, and He has commanded me to fear not.

Therefore, I will not let the spirit of fear overtake me, for I choose not to give fear any place in my life. I stand strong in faith, and I choose to believe God's Word instead of the lies of the enemy.

In God's Word I find peace, wisdom, and instruction for any situation. Because God is with me, God is for me, and God is in me, I have become fearless in my life. I am bold, strong, and very courageous. I am faith-filled and fear free.

Scripture Confessions

*Fear thou not; for I am with thee: be not dismayed;
for I am thy God: I will strengthen thee; yea, I will
help thee; yea, I will uphold thee with the right hand
of my righteousness.*

ISAIAH 41:10

*Yea, though I walk through the valley of the shadow
of death, I will fear no evil: for thou art with me; thy
rod and thy staff they comfort me.*

PSALM 23:4

*The LORD is my rock, and my fortress, and my
deliverer; my God, my strength, in whom I will
trust; my buckler, and the horn of my salvation, and
my high tower.*

PSALM 18:2

...I will never leave thee, nor forsake thee.

HEBREWS 13:5

*For God hath not given us the spirit of fear; but of
power, and of love, and of a sound mind.*

2 TIMOTHY 1:7

OVERCOMING WORRY

I cast my care, concern, and worry on the Lord. I refuse to worry or be fearful. I put my trust and confidence in God. God will take care of me because I know He loves me. I thank God for His presence and peace in my life. Jesus said not to let my heart be troubled or afraid, but to keep my mind focused on Him, knowing He will never leave me or forsake me.

God's Word says that the afflictions of the righteous are many, but He will deliver them out of them all. I will keep looking to God and not worry or be in fear about the circumstances of my life. God said that in this world I would have tribulation, but He told me to be of good cheer because He has overcome the world and will help me to do the same.

God's Word says not to take any thought about the future; therefore, I refuse to worry or be anxious concerning my future. I put my future in God's hands, and I know He will take care of me.

God's Word says that all things work together for good to those who love Him. I recognize that I can't do anything to change my circumstances by worrying, except to make them worse. What Satan has meant for evil, God will turn for good. I am free from worry, and I have victory in Jesus' name.

Scripture Confessions

Be careful for nothing; but in every thing by prayer and supplication with thanksgiving let your requests be made known unto God.

PHILIPPIANS 4:6

Casting all your care upon him; for he careth for you.

1 PETER 5:7

And the peace of God, which passeth all understanding, shall keep your hearts and minds through Christ Jesus.

PHILIPPIANS 4:7

These things I have spoken unto you, that in me ye might have peace. In the world ye shall have tribulation: but be of good cheer; I have overcome the world.

JOHN 16:33

OVERCOMING DISCOURAGEMENT

I will rejoice in the Lord and be glad because He loves me and cares for me. I refuse to be discouraged and I will not let my heart be troubled. I know that there is no problem too big, no hurt too deep, no mistake so bad that God's power, strength, and wisdom in me can't overcome it. I cast my cares, anxiety, and worries upon God. I will face adversity and tribulation with a courageous and cheerful heart. I am a world overcomer, and I refuse to be discouraged.

I fill my heart with praise and thanksgiving for all that God has done, is doing, and will do in my life. God has blessed me with so many wonderful blessings. I am determined to be patient in times of difficulty. I am determined to not give up, cave in, or quit when faced with adversity. I am strong and courageous in God. I will not allow discouragement to rear its ugly head.

The joy of the Lord is my strength. Anything the enemy has meant for evil in my life, God shall turn for good. I have hope, confidence, and faith that God will see me through any situation. I am strong and courageous in the Lord.

Scripture Confessions

Many are the afflictions of the righteous: but the LORD delivereth him out of them all.

PSALM 34:19

These things I have spoken unto you, that in me ye might have peace. In the world ye shall have tribulation: but be of good cheer; I have overcome the world.

JOHN 16:33

Then he said unto them, Go your way, eat the fat, and drink the sweet, and send portions unto them for whom nothing is prepared: for this day is holy unto our Lord: neither be ye sorry; for the joy of the LORD is your strength.

NEHEMIAH 8:10

But as for you, ye thought evil against me; but God meant it unto good, to bring to pass, as it is this day, to save much people alive.

GENESIS 50:20

IN TIMES OF ADVERSITY

The Lord is my rock, my fortress, and my strong tower. He is my provider and deliver. When troubles and adversity come my way I will not be fearful, worried, or full of anxiety. I am strong and confident in the Lord and will face adversity with undaunted courage. I will not be shaken because God is my strength and my ever present help in every situation.

He lifts me up and sustains me in the storms of this life. Even though the waves of adversity may beat upon my house, I will stand and not be destroyed because my life is built upon the rock of God's Word. Even though I may be surrounded with trouble and oppression, I will not be demoralized or succumb to the pressure to give up and quit. Even though I may suffer embarrassments and I am perplexed, I will not feel sorry for myself or be driven to despair, for my confidence is in God. Even though I might feel overwhelmed and see no way out, I will not give in to hopelessness, because the Lord is my salvation and my hope.

Even if I am persecuted, I know Jesus will stand with me and be my defender. He will never desert me or forsake me to stand alone. Even though I may be struck down to the ground, I will not be defeated or destroyed.

Many are the afflictions of the righteous: but the LORD delivereth him out of them all.

PSALM 34:19

But the salvation of the righteous is of the LORD: he is their strength in the time of trouble. And the LORD shall help them, and deliver them: he shall deliver them from the wicked, and save them, because they trust in him.

PSALM 37:39-40

These things I have spoken unto you, that in me ye might have peace. In the world ye shall have tribulation: but be of good cheer; I have overcome the world.

JOHN 16:33

We are troubled on every side, yet not distressed; we are perplexed, but not in despair; persecuted, but not forsaken; cast down, but not destroyed; always bearing about in the body the dying of the Lord Jesus, that the life also of Jesus might be made manifest in our body.

2 CORINTHIANS 4:8-10

...for he hath said, I will never leave thee, nor forsake thee.

HEBREWS 13:5

THE LORD IS MY REFUGE

The Lord is my rock, my fortress, and my deliverer, in whom I take refuge. He is my shield and my place of security. He is my refuge from the storms of this life. He is my dwelling place, and in His arms I am safe and secure. I find peace in His presence. He is my friend and my defender. His love for me is immeasurable. His heart is for me and not against me. Even when I have failed or I have done something wrong, His love draws me back to Him. His love and mercy are bigger than any sin in my life.

The Lord is my closest friend. When I am lonely, I find love and acceptance in His presence. I am always welcome to be in His presence. It is in His presence I find rest, I find understanding, I find comfort. He guides me and gives me insight when I am faced with decisions. He is an ever-present help in times of trouble. He knows me to the depths of my being and He still loves me unconditionally.

I am eager to hear His voice and I am willing to be obedient to Him. His Word is flawless, and He brings peace to my soul. His peace keeps me and His grace sustains me.

Scripture Confessions

As for God, his way is perfect; the word of the LORD is flawless. He is a shield for all who take refuge in him.

2 SAMUEL 22:31 NIV

The LORD is my rock, my fortress and my deliverer; my God is my rock, in whom I take refuge. He is my shield and the horn of my salvation, my stronghold.

PSALM 18:2 NIV

As for God, his way is perfect; the word of the LORD is flawless. He is a shield for all who take refuge in him.

PSALM 18:30 NIV

The LORD is good, a refuge in times of trouble. He cares for those who trust in him.

NAHUM 1:7 NIV

PEACE

God has given me His peace, not peace that comes from worldly sources, but a supernatural, divine peace. God's peace is a spiritual force that passes all natural reasoning and understanding. I will not allow my heart to be troubled, worried, or fearful, for I have God's peace in me. His peace keeps me cool, calm, and collected no matter what I am faced with. God's peace gives me the ability to remain level-headed and resolute in the face of misfortune and calamity.

His peace is the umpire of my soul; it garrisons and mounts guard over my heart and mind. God's peace keeps me from becoming fretful and anxious over situations in my life. He helps me to remain steady and unruffled when I face challenges and adversity. God's peace gives me confidence and surety that God is working for me, with me, and in me to fulfill His plan and purpose for my life. I can face the uncertainty of the future without apprehension and with complete confidence, knowing that God will work all things out for my good.

Scripture Confessions

Thou wilt keep him in perfect peace, whose mind is stayed on thee: because he trusteth in thee.

ISAIAH 26:3

For the mountains shall depart, and the hills be removed; but my kindness shall not depart from thee, neither shall the covenant of my peace be removed, saith the LORD that hath mercy on thee.

ISAIAH 54:10

Peace I leave with you, my peace I give unto you: not as the world giveth, give I unto you. Let not your heart be troubled, neither let it be afraid.

JOHN 14:27

And the peace of God, which passeth all understanding, shall keep your hearts and minds through Christ Jesus.

PHILIPPIANS 4:7

GUIDANCE FOR MY FUTURE

I will obey God's commands and fulfill His purpose for my life. I am committed to fulfilling God's will for my life. The Lord sees my every step and provides guidance for my life. I am full of His wisdom and discernment to make clear decisions. If I ever lack wisdom in any circumstance, I will ask God for wisdom, for He generously gives it to those who love Him. I am not alone in any situation. The Lord has provided me with His Spirit to lead, guide, and comfort me.

God's favor surrounds me like a shield. God is sending into my life the right people, the right friendships, and divine connections that will provide the support and guidance I need to fulfill God's specific will for my life. I am not worried or troubled about where I should be or what I should do. His peace fills my soul. I will seek first His kingdom and His righteousness, and all other things will be given to me. I will trust in the Lord with all my strength and He will make my paths straight.

I am not puzzled or worried about my future plans. I trust that this earth is God's and everything in it and that He will meet all of my needs.

Scripture Confessions

If any of you lacks wisdom, he should ask God, who give generously to all without finding fault, and it will be given him.

JAMES 1:5 NIV

Seek first his kingdom and his righteousness, and all these things will be given to you as well.

MATTHEW 6:33 NIV

Trust in the Lord with all your heart and lean not on your own understanding; in all your ways acknowledge him, and he will make your paths straight.

PROVERBS 3:5,6 NIV

"I know the plans I have for you," declares the Lord, "plans to prosper you and not to harm you, plans to give you hope and a future."

JEREMIAH 29:11 NIV

END THE DAY WITH GOD

I refuse to worry or carry any burdens concerning the activities of this day. I put all the events of this day behind me and refuse to be fearful or be anxious about anything I did or didn't do today. I cast all my cares on my heavenly Father.

I ask God to forgive me for any sin that I may have committed today. I receive God's forgiveness for my life and extend my forgiveness to anyone who may have sinned against me today.

God's grace is sufficient for every area of my life. His presence fills my soul. He is my refuge, my fortress, and my strong tower.

I choose not be fearful concerning tomorrow. I put my future, my hopes, and my dreams in God's hands. I trust Him to fulfill His plans and purposes in my life. He will sustain me, He will uphold me, He will deliver me from all my enemies. He has given me His peace that allows me to be calm, unruffled, and at rest even when faced with adversity and challenges.

God gives me sweet sleep. I will get a good night's sleep and wake up refreshed and revitalized ready for a new day.

Scripture Confessions

Casting all your care upon him; for he careth for you.

1 PETER 5:7

It is of the LORD's mercies that we are not consumed, because his compassions fail not. They are new every morning: great is thy faithfulness.

LAMENTATIONS 3:22-23

I will lie down peace and sleep in peace, for you alone, O LORD, make me dwell in safety.

PSALM 4:8 NIV

Personal Confessions

SCRIPTURE CONFESSIONS FOR SPIRITUAL GROWTH

START THE DAY WITH GOD

This is the day the Lord has made and I will rejoice and be glad in it. I make a conscious choice to let God's love, light, and life shine through me today. I am a child of God, and the Spirit of God lives in me. I am ready for anything and equal to anything because greater is He who is in me than he who is in the world.

God directs my steps today. I am spiritually keen, mentally alert, and physically strong. I am healed, healthy, and whole. I have a great attitude. I am determined to conduct my life in such a way that I will be a living witness to those around me. No matter what happens today, I know God will see me through.

Today is going to be a great day. Blessings of abundance, health, and favor are coming my way. I am confident, fearless, and courageous. I will fulfill God's plan and purpose for my life. I am on track, in step, and right on the mark concerning God's perfect will for me. I am not easily distracted but focused, disciplined, and committed to fulfill the destiny that God has for me.

Scripture Confessions

This is the day which the LORD hath made; we will rejoice and be glad in it.

PSALM 118:24

It is of the LORD's mercies that we are not consumed, because his compassions fail not. They are new every morning: great is thy faithfulness.

LAMENTATIONS 3:22,23

In all thy ways acknowledge him, and he shall direct thy paths.

PROVERBS 3:6

I can do all things through Christ which strengtheneth me.

PHILIPPIANS 4:13

What shall we then say to these things? If God be for us, who can be against us?

ROMANS 8:31

I HAVE BEEN
RECONCILED TO GOD

I have been reconciled to God through Jesus Christ my Savior. I am now in a favored position. Jesus came that I might have abundant life through His blood. He purchased my reconciliation. I am in agreement with God's will for my life. I am now in the family of God. God is now my heavenly Father. He chose me, He adopted me, He loved me so much He sent His Son to die for me to redeem me. I am no longer a servant but a child of God. He has given me His love, grace, and mercy. I am complete in Him.

My past is past; God has forgiven me and has pardoned me. Though my sins were once as scarlet, I am now white as snow. Through my union with Him, I have the power to live a life of peace, a life of joy, and a life of victory. It's not by my works but through the shed blood of Jesus that I have been redeemed, restored, and reconciled to God.

Scripture Confessions

I have swept away your offenses like a cloud, your sins like the morning mist. Return to me, for I have redeemed you.

ISAIAH 44:22 NIV

Now he has reconciled you by Christ's physical body through death to present you holy in his sight, without blemish and free from accusation.

COLOSSIANS 1:22 NIV

"Come now, let us reason together," says the LORD. "Though your sins are like scarlet, they shall be as white as snow; though they are red as crimson, they shall be like wool."

ISAIAH 1:18 NIV

I AM AN AMBASSADOR OF GOD

I am an ambassador of God's kingdom. I will represent my Father and my Savior with honor, integrity, and dignity. I will live a life of purity and holiness before God and before my fellow man. I am an ambassador of God's love; I am an ambassador of His peace and I am an ambassador of His mercy. I am quick to forgive the mistakes and shortcomings of others. I am understanding, kind, and I am not angered easily. I am an ambassador of God's healing power. I am an ambassador of the power and might of the Holy Spirit. I am calm, cool, and collected. Even when I encounter adverse circumstances, I will respond to every situation with His wisdom, His ability, and His insight. As an ambassador of the Most High God, I will endeavor to conduct my life at all times in a manner that will be pleasing to Him. I will represent the Christian Faith with truth, integrity, and excellence.

So we are Christ's ambassadors, God making His appeal as it were through us. We [as Christ's personal representatives] beg you for His sake to lay hold of the divine favor [now offered you] and be reconciled to God.

2 Corinthians 5:20 AMP

Love is patient, love is kind. It does not envy, it does not boast, it is not proud. It is not rude, it is not selfseeking, it is not easily angered, it keeps no record of wrongs. Love does not delight in evil but rejoices with the truth. It always protects, always trusts, always hopes, always perseveres. Love never fails.

1 Corinthians 13:4-8 NIV

My mouth shall speak of wisdom; and the meditation of my heart shall be of understanding.

Psalm 49:3

I Am Free from the Law of Sin and Death

The Spirit of Life has broken the chains of satanic bondage over my life. Satan no longer has control or influence in my life. The law of the Spirit of life in Christ Jesus has made me free from the law of sin and death. The Spirit of Life is now the dominating force in my life. The Holy Spirit empowers me, makes me strong, and gives me life. I now have strength, courage and spiritual authority to resist the devil and his influences.

I am no longer a slave to the devil. I am no longer bound or controlled by the forces of darkness; they have no hold on me. I am free from Satan and his bondages. I am free from sickness and disease. I am free from poverty and lack. I am free from worry and anxiety. I am free from death and destruction. I am free from fear and evil entanglements. I am free from depression and despair. I am free from sinful addictions. I am determined to live my life in complete and total freedom and victory. I am free in Christ Jesus and I am enjoying living free in Him

Scripture Confessions

The law of the Spirit of life [which is] in Christ Jesus [the law of our new being] has freed me from the law of sin and death.

ROMANS 8:2 AMP

It is for freedom that Christ has set us free. Stand firm, then, and do not let yourselves be burdened again by a yoke of slavery.

GALATIANS 5:1 NIV

Where the Spirit of the Lord is, there is freedom.

2 CORINTHIANS 3:17 NIV

I AM THE RIGHTEOUSNESS OF GOD

Second Corinthians 5:21 says that we have been made the righteousness of God. Therefore, in obedience to God's Word, I boldly confess that I am the righteousness of God in Christ. This is not by my goodness, not because I am holy within myself but because, through the shed blood of Jesus my Savior, I have been made righteous and acceptable in the sight of my heavenly Father. To be righteous means to be in right standing with God. That's why I can go boldly into the throne room and obtain grace and mercy. I am righteous not because of what I have done but because of what Jesus has done for me. His righteousness is His gift to me.

Scripture Confessions

For our sake He made Christ [virtually] to be sin Who knew no sin, so that in and through Him we might become [endued with, viewed as being in, and examples of] the righteousness of God [what we ought to be, approved and acceptable and in right relationship with Him, by His goodness].

2 CORINTHIANS 5:21 AMP

As by one man's disobedience many were made sinners, so by the obedience of one shall many be made righteous.

ROMANS 5:19

Let us therefore come boldly unto the throne of grace, that we may obtain mercy, and find grace to help in time of need.

HEBREWS 4:16

I AM CHOSEN OF GOD

I am chosen of God, I am part of His chosen generation. I am a peculiar person, set apart for God's causes and purpose. He has made me a part of His royal priesthood. He has called me out of darkness and now I live in His marvelous light because of what Jesus did. I have dominion and authority in the realm of the Spirit. Satan is under my feet. He has no power over me. Sickness and disease, poverty and lack have no authority over me. Through the power of the blood of Jesus I take my place as a prophet, priest, and king over all the affairs of my life.

Ye are a chosen generation, a royal priesthood, an holy nation, a peculiar people; that ye should shew forth the praises of him who hath called you out of darkness into his marvellous light.

1 PETER 2:9

To him who loves us and has freed us from our sins by his blood, and has made us to be a kingdom and priests to serve his God and Father—to him be glory and power for ever and ever! Amen.

REVELATION 1:6 NIV

You were once darkness, but now you are light in the Lord. Live as children of light.

EPHESIANS 5:8 NIV

NOTHING CAN SEPARATE ME FROM GOD'S LOVE

God loved me so much that He sent His only Son, Jesus, to die for me. Jesus took my place. He took the burden and anguish of my sin so I wouldn't have to. He was my substitute. His love for me was the driving force that caused Him to endure the cross. He is merciful, kind, and forgiving. His love has no limits; He never condemns me but always reaches out to me. He loves me unconditionally. He is concerned about every aspect of my life.

God's love for me is greater than any sin I have committed, greater than any failure I have had. God's love for me is an unchangeable fact of this universe. Nothing I do, nothing people do, nothing the devil does can separate me from God's love. Not death, not life, not angels or principalities—nothing can separate me from His love. God's love for me is eternal. His love knows no boundaries; it never gives up believing in me or reaching out to me. His love comforts me, His love sustains me, and His love encourages my soul and restores my hope. God's love endures forever.

Scripture Confessions

I am persuaded, that neither death, nor life, nor angels, nor principalities, nor powers, nor things present, nor things to come, nor height, nor depth, nor any other creature, shall be able to separate us from the love of God, which is in Christ Jesus our Lord.

ROMANS 8:38,39

God so loved the world that he gave his one and only Son, that whoever believes in him shall not perish but have eternal life.

JOHN 3:16 NIV

Give thanks to the LORD, for he is good; his love endures forever.

1 CHRONICLES 16:34 NIV

BEING A GODLY PERSON

I have God's wisdom and insight in all the matters of my life. I am determined to have God's character developed in me. I will allow God's love, life, and light to shine through me. I am in agreement with God's Word and I boldly confess that I am strong in the Lord and in the power of His might. I put a guard over my mouth so that I never criticize or condemn. I will never say or do anything that would erode another person's confidence or self-image.

I will walk in love and manifest the fruit of God's Spirit on a daily basis. I will be quick to listen and slow to speak. My friends will find a receptive and understanding heart in me.

By prayer and praise I will create an atmosphere of God's presence in my life. I am keen and sensitive to the voice of the Holy Spirit and I am quick to obey whatever He tells me to do.

I put God's Word as first priority in my life; it is the standard and cornerstone of all my decisions.

The truth and principles of God's Word are my benchmarks for every decision. God's Word is my guiding light, providing guidance and direction. I will meditate on God's Word day and night and do my best to obey its instructions. I am determined to live a life that is honorable and pleasing to the Lord.

Scripture Confessions

The fruit of the Spirit is love, joy, peace, longsuffering, gentleness, goodness, faith, meekness, temperance: against such there is no law.

GALATIANS 5:22,23

His delight is in the law of the LORD; and in his law doth he meditate day and night.

PSALM 1:2

With my whole heart have I sought thee: O let me not wander from thy commandments. Thy word have I hid in mine heart, that I might not sin against thee.

PSALM 119:10-11

FORGIVENESS

I choose to forgive any individual who has hurt me in the past. As an act of my will, I forgive them for what they did. I will not hate them, despise them, or desire that they suffer retribution for their actions. I give all the hurt and bitterness in my life to God. I refuse to carry the burden of those past hurts in my heart anymore. My heart is cleansed by God's Word. I release the individuals who have hurt me, I will no longer live with the suffered wrong or harbor any ill will towards anyone. I will not gossip about what they did or ridicule or attack their character. Instead, I choose to obey God's Word, which tells me to let go of the past and press on toward the future. Most of all, I forgive myself for every failure, every mistake, every stupid decision, for anything I have ever done that brought pain or disappointment to another person

God forgave me of all my transgressions and I choose to do the same. I am free from the clutches of unforgiveness. I will not let the pain of my past rob me of the promise of my future.

Scripture Confessions

And forgive us our debts, as we forgive our debtors.

MATTHEW 6:12

Remember ye not the former things, neither consider the things of old.

ISAIAH 43:18

Brethren, I count not myself to have apprehended: but this one thing I do, forgetting those things which are behind, and reaching forth unto those things which are before, I press toward the mark for the prize of the high calling of God in Christ Jesus.

PHILIPPIANS 3:13-14

If we confess our sins, he is faithful and just and will forgive us our sins and purify us from all unrighteousness.

1 JOHN 1:9 NIV

I AM SPIRITUALLY MINDED

I am determined to be spiritually minded every day. I will not let the negative influences of this world pollute my mind. I will put God's Word first and I will meditate on it day and night. I will confess God's promises over my life, and I will pray in the Spirit. My life pleases God and I am full of His life and peace. I am in control of my mind.

I will not gossip or listen to gossip about others. I will not listen to music that is not edifying. I will not watch TV or DVD's that are full of sinful junk that brings my spirit down. I will not engage in conversations with others who criticize, condemn, and complain. I choose to keep my mind free from the entanglements of this life and I choose to think on good things.

Scripture Confessions

But we have the mind of Christ (the Messiah) and do hold the thoughts (feelings and purposes) of His heart.

1 CORINTHIANS 2:16 AMP

But seek first his kingdom and his righteousness, and all these things will be given to you as well.

MATTHEW 6:33 NIV

Finally, brothers, whatever is true, whatever is noble, whatever is right, whatever is pure, whatever is lovely, whatever is admirable—if anything is excellent or praiseworthy—think about such things.

PHILIPPIANS 4:8 NIV

HEARING GOD'S VOICE

God's Word says I am His child and I know His voice. Therefore, I proclaim that I know God's voice and I will not be deceived by the voice of the enemy. I am sensitive to the voice of the Holy Spirit and I am obedient to His instruction, direction, and guidance. I am tuned in to the Holy Spirit and I am keen to hear His voice. I am mindful not to do anything that grieves the Holy Spirit. I am diligent to spend time in prayer, fellowship, and worship with the Lord so that I continually keep myself in proper spiritual condition to hear His voice.

I seek His wisdom and counsel concerning all matters of my life. He is faithful to speak to me concerning changes or corrections I need to make. I am faithful to do everything He would have me to do. He speaks to me through His Word. As I study and meditate on the Scriptures, their life-giving force gives me spiritual strength. God's Word enlightens my spirit and illuminates my mind. My union with Him grows stronger every day as I grow in my ability to hear His voice clearly and accurately.

Scripture Confessions

This thing commanded I them, saying, Obey my voice, and I will be your God, and ye shall be my people: and walk ye in all the ways that I have commanded you, that it may be well unto you.

JEREMIAH 7:23

When he putteth forth his own sheep, he goeth before them, and the sheep follow him: for they know his voice. And a stranger will they not follow, but will flee from him: for they know not the voice of strangers.

JOHN 10:4-5

My sheep hear my voice, and I know them, and they follow me.

JOHN 10:27

So then faith cometh by hearing, and hearing by the word of God.

ROMANS 10:17

SPEAKING THE RIGHT WORDS

I put a guard over my mouth. I choose to speak words of life, health, and healing. I choose to speak only words that are gracious and kind.

I will not speak evil of any person. I will not gossip or spread rumors. I will not speak words of death, destruction, or discouragement. I will be mindful to speak words that encourage, uplift, and inspire others. I refuse to criticize, condemn, or complain.

I refuse to give in to the temptation to speak before I think. I refuse to speak the wrong words when I am frustrated or angry. I choose to not be sarcastic, facetious, or condescending in my communication to others.

I put God's Word in my mouth, and I speak His promises over my life and the lives of others throughout the day. I am sensitive to the needs of others. I am quick to speak words of comfort, peace, and kindness to everyone I meet. My words bring hope, faith, and encouragement to all who hear them.

Scripture Confessions

By thy words thou shalt be justified, and by thy words thou shalt be condemned.

MATTHEW 12:37

Put on therefore, as the elect of God, holy and beloved, bowels of mercies, kindness, humbleness of mind, meekness, longsuffering; forbearing one another, and forgiving one another, if any man have a quarrel against any: even as Christ forgave you, so also do ye. And above all these things put on charity, which is the bond of perfectness.

COLOSSIANS 3:12-14

Let no corrupt communication proceed out of your mouth, but that which is good to the use of edifying, that it may minister grace unto the hearers.

EPHESIANS 4:29

PSALM 23

The Lord is my shepherd, my keeper, my protector. He watches over me. He cares about every little thing that affects my life. I shall not want or lack for anything. He gives me rest and peace in my life even in the middle of a world of turmoil. He refreshes and restores my life. He is a breath of fresh air to my soul. He is my guide in my new life of righteousness.

Even though I may walk through a dark valley and feel like death is all around me, I will not fear or be in despair for God is with me. He said He would never leave or forsake me. His love and protection surround my life like a shield. He will allow no harm or evil to befall me. His strength and guidance sustain me in troubled times.

God is always blessing me and giving me good things. God blesses me so much that it makes my enemies jealous. His goodness, mercy, and lovingkindness will follow me all the days of my life. My daily quest is to live in His presence.

Scripture Confessions

The LORD is my strength and my shield; my heart trusts in him, and I am helped.

PSALM 28:7 NIV

He satisfies the thirsty and fills the hungry with good things.

PSALM 107:9 NIV

Surely goodness and mercy shall follow me all the days of my life: and I will dwell in the house of the LORD for ever.

PSALM 23:6

END THE DAY WITH GOD

Iam thankful for another day. I refuse to worry or carry any burdens concerning the activities of this day. I cast all my cares on my heavenly Father. I put all the events of this day behind me and refuse to be fearful or be anxious about anything I did or didn't do today.

I ask God to forgive me for any sin I may have committed today. I receive God's forgiveness and extend my forgiveness to anyone who may have offended me today.

God's grace is sufficient for every area of my life. His presence fills my soul. He is my refuge, my fortress, and my strong tower.

I choose not to be fearful concerning tomorrow. I put my future, my hopes, and my dreams in God's hands. I trust Him to fulfill His plans and purposes in my life. He will sustain me, He will uphold me, He will deliver me from all my enemies. God's supernatural peace refreshes and restores my soul.

God gives me sweet sleep. I will get a good night's sleep and wake up refreshed and revitalized, ready for a new day.

Scripture Confessions

Casting all your care upon him; for he careth for you.
1 PETER 5:7

It is of the LORD's mercies that we are not consumed, because his compassions fail not. They are new every morning: great is thy faithfulness.
LAMENTATIONS 3:22-23

I will lie down and sleep in peace, for you alone, O LORD, make me dwell in safety.
PSALM 4:8 NIV

Personal Confessions

_____

_____

_____

_____

_____

_____

_____

_____

_____

_____

_____

_____

_____

_____

_____

SCRIPTURE CONFESSIONS FOR HEALING

START THE DAY WITH GOD FOR HEALING

This is the day that the Lord has made, and I will rejoice and be glad in it. I start every day with God by speaking life, health, strength, and vitality into my body because I know God's healing power is at work within me. The nature and life of God are resident in my body, driving out all manner of sickness and disease. I am strong in the Lord and in the power of His might. I believe the Word of God above anything that I think, feel, or see. His Word says that I have been redeemed from the curse of sickness. His Word says that by Jesus' stripes I am healed.

My body is free from pain, sickness, and disease. It operates effectively and efficiently—free from malfunction of any kind. Every part of my body is functioning properly. Every organ, gland, and system is operating in conjunction with each other in perfect harmony, which is exactly how God designed my body to work. My immune system is strong, vibrant, and healthy. Germs, bacteria, viruses, and parasites cannot exist in my body. If any sickness or disease makes any attempt to try and attack my body, then it is quickly destroyed by the power of God's Word working in me. I boldly declare that I am healed, healthy, and whole.

Scripture Confessions

He was wounded for our transgressions, he was bruised for our iniquities: the chastisement of our peace was upon him; and with his stripes we are healed.

ISAIAH 53:5

Be strong in the Lord, and in the power of his might.

EPHESIANS 6:10

Christ hath redeemed us from the curse of the law, being made a curse for us: for it is written, Cursed is every one that hangeth on a tree.

GALATIANS 3:13

HEALING

I proclaim healing for my body. By Jesus' stripes, I was healed. The healing, life-giving, diseasedestroying power of God is working in my body. It drives out all manner of sickness and disease. I am full of life, health, strength, and vitality. I am healthy and whole from the top of my head to the soles of my feet. Every organ in my body operates and functions the way God created it with no disease or malfunctions. Every system in my body operates and functions with supernatural efficiency. My nervous system, lymphatic system, digestive system, electrical system, circulatory system, and every other system functions with 100 percent efficiency.

Jesus Himself bore my sickness and carried my diseases; therefore, sickness and disease are not allowed to exist in my body. My body is free from growths, tumors, or obstructions of any kind.

The divine zoe-life of God flows through me, quickening and making alive my mortal body. My body is free from pain, discomfort, distress, and all symptoms of sickness. God's Word is medicine to my flesh. I am not moved by how I feel, how I look, or any negative reports, because I believe God's Word and His Word says I am healed. I am healed, healthy, and whole in Jesus' name.

Scripture Confessions

But he was wounded for our transgressions, he was bruised for our iniquities: the chastisement of our peace was upon him; and with his stripes we are healed.

ISAIAH 53:5

My son, attend to my words; incline thine ear unto my sayings. Let them not depart from thine eyes; keep them in the midst of thine heart. For they are life unto those that find them, and health to all their flesh.

PROVERBS 4:20-22

He sent his word, and healed them, and delivered them from their destructions.

PSALM 107:20

That it might be fulfilled which was spoken by Esaias the prophet, saying, Himself took our infirmities, and bare our sicknesses.

MATTHEW 8:17

Who his own self bare our sins in his own body on the tree, that we, being dead to sins, should live unto righteousness: by whose stripes ye were healed.

1 PETER 2:24

HEALTHY LIFESTYLE

According to Romans 12:1, in obedience to God's Word, I present myself to God as a living sacrifice. My body is the temple of the Holy Spirit. I choose to honor God by taking care of my body. I will not defile my body by eating or drinking anything that causes harm to me in any way.

I am strong in my convictions, and with the Holy Spirit's help I will not give in to the temptation of my flesh. I am strong in the Lord and the power of His might. I walk in the Spirit, and therefore, I will not fulfill the lust of my flesh. I refuse to let the desires of my flesh control my eating habits. I will not eat health-destroying foods or substances.

I am disciplined in my body; I will exercise every day and drink plenty of water. I will discipline my life so that I obtain optimum performance mentally, physically, and spiritually. I will not abuse my body by not getting enough sleep. I choose to be sensitive to the needs of my body and will make healthy choices regarding my lifestyle that will cause me to function with the highest efficiency. I will make quality life decisions regarding my spiritual, mental, and physical fitness and well-being.

I beseech you therefore, brethren, by the mercies of God, that ye present your bodies a living sacrifice, holy, acceptable unto God, which is your reasonable service.

ROMANS 12:1

This I say then, Walk in the Spirit, and ye shall not fulfil the lust of the flesh.

GALATIANS 5:16

OVERCOMING FATIGUE

I am strong in the Lord and the power of His might. I refuse to let the cares of this life burden me down with weariness and fatigue. The same Spirit that raised Christ Jesus from the dead lives in me and makes alive my mortal body.

The joy of the Lord is my strength. My youth is renewed like the eagle's. When I am weary, He makes me strong. I shall walk and not be weary, and I shall run and not faint. In the Lord's presence my soul is renewed and my mental and physical strength is restored. The Spirit of the Most High lives in me and His anointing energizes me. As a result, fatigue and weariness vanish from my body.

I draw strength from God's Word. I am refreshed and revitalized by the power of the Holy Spirit. I am alive with His divine nature and resurrection life. The life of God flows in my body, and I have strength for all things. My body is strong, vibrant, and full of the life. I am well, healthy, and strong. My body is full of vitality, energy, and power. My soul is at peace, my body is refreshed, and my spirit is strong in the Lord.

Scripture Confessions

Cast thy burden upon the LORD, and he shall sustain thee: he shall never suffer the righteous to be moved.

PSALM 55:22

Who satisfieth thy mouth with good things; so that thy youth is renewed like the eagle's.

PSALM 103:5

What? know ye not that your body is the temple of the Holy Ghost which is in you, which ye have of God, and ye are not your own?

1 CORINTHIANS 6:19

And let us not be weary in well doing: for in due season we shall reap, if we faint not.

GALATIANS 6:9

I know both how to be abased, and I know how to abound: every where and in all things I am instructed both to be full and to be hungry, both to abound and to suffer need. I can do all things through Christ which strengtheneth me.

PHILIPPANS 4:12-13

But they that wait upon the LORD shall renew their strength; they shall mount up with wings as eagles; they shall run, and not be weary; they shall walk, and not faint.

ISAIAH 40:31

Supernatural Strength

I am strong in the Lord and in the power of His might. The joy of the Lord is my strength, and His strength sustains me. I am full of energy; I am vibrant and full of life and vitality. God in me is stronger than any weakness in my flesh. It doesn't matter how I feel because I am not moved by feelings. I speak supernatural strength, energy, and vitality to my body. Weakness, tiredness, and weariness, I command you to get out of my body.

I can do all things through Christ who strengthens me. I have dynamic energy and indomitable strength. I am undaunted in my faith; I am strong in the Lord. I am courageous and fearless.

Greater is He that is in me than he that is in the world. God's strength rises up in me; He puts me above my feelings. I am strong in my spirit, I am strong in my mind, and I am strong in my body.

My strength is renewed like the eagle's. God increases my strength; therefore, I am not weary.

Scripture Confessions

The joy of the LORD is your strength.

NEHEMIAH 8:10

I can do all things through Christ which strengtheneth me.

PHILIPPIANS 4:13

Greater is he that is in you, than he that is in the world.

1 JOHN 4:4

Bless the LORD...who satisfieth thy mouth with good things; so that thy youth is renewed like the eagle's.

PSALM 103:1,5

He gives power to the weak, And to those who have no might He increases strength.

ISAIAH 40:29 NKJV

Be strong and courageous! ...Do not be afraid or discouraged, for the LORD will personally go ahead of you. He will be with you; he will neither fail you nor abandon you.

DEUTERONOMY 31:7,8 NLT

I WILL NOT GIVE UP

Even though I may be surrounded by oppressors, I am never smothered or crushed by them. I may suffer embarrassments and become perplexed, and it may seem that there is no way out, but I still will not be driven to despair. Even though I may be pursued, persecuted, and hard driven, God will never desert me and make me stand alone. Even though I may be struck down to the ground, I will never be struck out or destroyed. No matter what difficulties or obstacles may come my way, I will never, never, never quit!

I will not faint in the time of adversity because God is with me. I am strong and very courageous. I am persistent and undaunted in my faith. I shall never quit and I will not yield. I will not bow my knee to sickness. I am steadfast and unmovable. I am valiant and fearless, determined and resolute in my faith. I am strong in the Lord and in the power of His might. No weapon formed against me shall prosper. I will not lose heart; I will not weaken or cave in. Victory is mine. I am relentless in my pursuit of total and complete wellness and wholeness for my body.

Thou shalt make thy way prosperous, and then thou shalt have good success. Have not I commanded thee? Be strong and of a good courage.

JOSHUA 1:8-9

[The Lord said] I will never leave thee, nor forsake thee.

HEBREWS 13:5

For only we who believe can enter his rest.

HEBREWS 4:3 NLT

We are hedged in (pressed) on every side [troubled and oppressed in every way], but not cramped or crushed; we suffer embarrassments and are perplexed and unable to find a way out, but not driven to despair; We are pursued (persecuted and hard driven), but not deserted [to stand alone]; we are struck down to the ground, but never struck out and destroyed; Always carrying about in the body the liability and exposure to the same putting to death that the Lord Jesus suffered, so that the [resurrection] life of Jesus also may be shown forth by and in our bodies.

2 CORINTHIANS 4:8-10 AMP

Jesus Already Did It!

Matthew 8:17 declares that Jesus Himself bore my sicknesses and diseases. And since He already bore them, I don't have to. He was made sick so that I might be made well. He was beaten and bruised for me. He was my substitute, and He became sick so I wouldn't have to.

First Peter 2:24 says by His stripes I was healed. That is past tense. If I was healed, then that means that healing is already mine today. All I have to do is receive it. My healing was a gift from my Lord and Savior. Jesus did it for me. He was bruised for my iniquities, the chastisement of my peace was on Him, and by His stripes I am healed.

My healing was bought and paid for two thousand years ago. I am not sick and trying to get healed. I am already healed, and sickness is trying to take hold in my body. But I won't let it! I boldly proclaim that Jesus already did it! Therefore, I am healed! Sickness has no right to stay in my body. I am healed, healthy, and whole in the mighty name of Jesus.

Scripture Confessions

Surely he hath borne our griefs, and carried our sorrows: yet we did esteem him stricken, smitten of God, and afflicted. But he was wounded for our transgressions, he was bruised for our iniquities: the chastisement of our peace was upon him; and with his stripes we are healed.

ISAIAH 53:4-5

Bless the LORD, O my soul, and forget not all his benefits: Who forgiveth all thine iniquities; who healeth all thy diseases; who redeemeth thy life from destruction; who crowneth thee with lovingkindness and tender mercies.

PSALM 103:2-4

For he hath made him to be sin for us, who knew no sin; that we might be made the righteousness of God in him.

2 CORINTHIANS 5:21

REDEEMED FROM THE CURSE

Galatians 3:13 says I have been redeemed from the curse of the law. That means that the law of life in Christ Jesus has set me free from the law of sin and death. Sickness is a curse, and by the power of the redemptive blood of Jesus Christ, the Anointed One, I have been set free from the curse of sickness. Sickness, you have no right to stay in my body. The chains and bonds of sickness and disease have been broken over my life. Through Christ Jesus, they have no power to hurt or harm me. I am free from their bondage and captivity because Jesus was made sick so that I might be made well. I am a child of the Most High God, and healing is the bread of God's children.

The curse has been broken through the redemptive work of Jesus. Abraham's blessings are also mine, and they include health and healing for my body. So as I have been redeemed from the curse, it no longer has any power over me. Jesus has given me power, dominion, and authority over sickness and disease. I choose to exercise that authority and boldly proclaim that I am free of sickness and disease, and I walk in health, healing, and wholeness. I am strong, healthy, and full of strength and vitality—and I have been redeemed from the curse.

Scripture Confessions

Christ hath redeemed us from the curse of the law, being made a curse for us; for it is written, Cursed is every one that hangeth on a tree.

GALATIANS 3:13

The law of the Spirit of life in Christ Jesus hath made me free from the law of sin and death.

ROMANS 8:2

In whom we have redemption through his blood, the forgiveness of sins, according to the riches of his grace.

EPHESIANS 1:7

ORGANS, SYSTEMS, AND GLANDS

I speak to every organ in my body and command all of them to operate and function at 100 percent efficiency, the way God made them. My heart is strong and healthy, every valve working in perfect harmony. My heart beats in perfect rhythm, all the blood vessels surrounding my heart are free from blockages of any kind. My liver, kidneys, and lungs all operate and function effectively and efficiently with no hindrances. All my organs function and perform their duties effectively. All my organs are healthy and whole—free from sickness, disease, growths, and tumors.

Every system in my body operates like a welloiled machine. My nervous system, my electrical system, my circulatory system, my lymphatic system, my digestive system, and every other system operate in total and complete harmony with each other. They are free from sickness, disease, growths, or tumors of any kind.

I speak life and health to all the glands in my body. I proclaim that they are healthy and whole. My adrenal gland, thyroid gland, pituitary gland, and all other glands in my body operate and function at 100 percent efficiency—free from sickness, disease, growths, and tumors. My body is healed, healthy, and whole; I am full of vim, vigor, and vitality.

Scripture Confessions

He sent his word, and healed them, and delivered them from their destructions.

PSALM 107:20

And ye shall serve the LORD your God, and he shall bless thy bread, and thy water; and I will take sickness away from the midst of thee.

EXODUS 23:25

But if the Spirit of him that raised up Jesus from the dead dwell in you, he that raised up Christ from the dead shall also quicken your mortal bodies by his Spirit that dwelleth in you.

ROMANS 8:11

When You Receive
A Bad Report

I am not shaken because of bad reports; I choose to believe the Lord's good report. Bad news doesn't faze me a bit because I have learned to trust God and believe His Word even in the midst of challenging circumstances. I don't deny that sickness exists; I just deny it has a right to exist in my body.

The word of men doesn't change the Word of God. I don't deny what the doctor's word says; I just deny that it is the final word, because God's Word supersedes the word of men. I choose to believe God's report that says Jesus paid for my healing as my substitute on the Cross. His report says the law of life in Christ Jesus has made me free from the law of sin and death. His report says that healing and health are my right and privilege. God's Word says that by Jesus' stripes I was healed, and that is the report I choose to believe. It doesn't matter what the doctor says; I am healed. It doesn't matter what the medical tests say; I am healed. It doesn't matter what my body says; I say I am healed. God's Word says that I am healed, and I believe it. That settles the matter.

Scripture Confessions

So shall my word be that goeth forth out of my mouth: it shall not return unto me void, but it shall accomplish that which I please, and it shall prosper in the thing whereto I sent it.

ISAIAH 55:11

That it might be fulfilled which was spoken by Esaias the prophet, saying, Himself took our infirmities, and bare our sicknesses.

MATTHEW 8:17

Finally, brethren, whatever things are true, whatever things are noble, whatever things are just, whatever things are pure, whatever things are lovely, whatever things are of good report, if there is any virtue and if there is anything praiseworthy— meditate on these things.

PHILIPPIANS 4:8 NKJV

OVERCOMING FEAR

I am strong and very courageous; I will not fear. I will not let fear impact my life. I am not afraid, because God's Word gives me boldness and audacity. I do not fear the devil, I fear no sickness, I fear no disease. I am not intimidated by sickness and disease, but they are intimidated by my faith in God's Word. My faith and trust in God and His Word destroys the power of fear. God has not given me a spirit of fear but of power and love and a sound mind.

I refuse to get stressed out; I refuse to worry or be anxious. I stand firm and fearless in my faith. I will not fear because God is for me, God is with me, and God is in me. When God is for me, then nothing can be against me. Because God is in me, I can conquer anything. I am bold in my faith and I refuse to let one ounce of fear enter my life. I shall not be afraid, for the Lord is my God. I shall not fear, because my confidence is in the Lord. No fear here, in Jesus' name!

Scripture Confessions

Be strong and of a good courage.

JOSHUA 1:6

David said to Solomon his son, Be strong and of good courage, and do it: fear not, nor be dismayed: for the LORD God...will not fail thee.

1 CHRONICLES 28:20

Fear thou not; for I am with thee.

ISAIAH 41:10

God hath not given us the spirit of fear; but of power, and of love, and of a sound mind.

2 TIMOTHY 1:7

Peace I leave with you, my peace I give unto you: not as the world giveth, give I unto you. Let not your heart be troubled, neither let it be afraid.

JOHN 14:27

As soon as Jesus heard the word that was spoken, he saith unto the ruler of the synagogue, Be not afraid, only believe.

MARK 5:36

AUTHORITY OVER SATAN

Jesus came that I may have abundant life, but Satan comes to steal, kill, and destroy. God's will for my life is health and wholeness. Satan's will for my life is destruction, disease, and death. I choose abundant life. I remind you, Satan, that Jesus has already defeated you and taken away your authority to harm me. And it's in His name that I boldly proclaim: Satan, you are under my feet. I resist you, and I stand steadfast in my faith. I expect you to turn tail and run the other way. In the name of Jesus, I command you to stop and desist in any and all attempts to put sickness or disease on my body.

I take authority over Satan and break the power of any curses or spells that have been spoken over my life. Witchcraft, black magic, and all the forces of darkness have no power to affect my body. I cast down and break the power of any strategies, maneuvers, or evil plots that the enemy has set in motion to bring destruction to my life. They shall all come to naught because no weapon formed against me will prosper!

Scripture Confessions

The thief cometh not, but for to steal, and to kill, and to destroy: I am come that they might have life, and that they might have it more abundantly.

JOHN 10:10

No weapon that is formed against thee shall prosper.

ISAIAH 54:17

...I have set before you life and death, blessing and cursing: therefore choose life, that both thou and thy seed may live.

DEUTERONOMY 30:19

...He gave them power and authority to drive out all demons and to cure diseases.

LUKE 9:1 NIV

Submit yourselves therefore to God. Resist the devil, and he will flee from you.

JAMES 4:7

But thanks be to God, which giveth us the victory through our Lord Jesus Christ. Therefore, my beloved brethren, be ye stedfast, unmoveable, always abounding in the work of the Lord, forasmuch as ye know that your labour is not in vain in the Lord.

1 CORINTHIANS 15:57-58

SPEAK TO THE MOUNTAIN

My words have power. Jesus said if I would speak to a mountain in my life and tell it to be plucked up and thrown into the sea it would have to obey me. So because Jesus said to do it, and because I am obedient to His commands, I speak to the mountain of sickness in my life.

Sickness, listen up, pay attention. I am talking to you! In the name of Jesus Christ, the Anointed One, I command you to be plucked up and thrown out of my life and body. You have no choice. You can't stay. You have to leave. There is no alternative, no other options. Pack your bags, hit the road, and don't come back anymore. Today's mountain is tomorrow's testimony. It doesn't matter how big the mountain is, and it doesn't matter how long the mountain has been there. What does matter is what Jesus says about the mountain. He said if I speak to the mountain, it has to obey me. My life is mountain free—no mountains of sickness and disease here. The mountain of sickness has been eradicated and eliminated from my life. I am healed, healthy, and whole in Jesus' name.

Scripture Confessions

Whosoever shall say unto this mountain, Be thou removed, and be thou cast into the sea; and shall not doubt in his heart, but shall believe that those things which he saith shall come to pass; he shall have whatsoever he saith.

MARK 11:23

So Jesus said to them, "Because of your unbelief; for assuredly, I say to you, if you have faith as a mustard seed, you will say to this mountain, 'Move from here to there,' and it will move; and nothing will be impossible for you."

MATTHEW 17:20 NKJV

And I will give unto thee the keys of the kingdom of heaven: and whatsoever thou shalt bind on earth shall be bound in heaven: and whatsoever thou shalt loose on earth shall be loosed in heaven.

MATTHEW 16:19

END THE DAY WITH GOD FOR HEALING

The Spirit of the Lord is on me. He quickens me and gives me strength. In Him I find rest, comfort, and peace. Even in the midst of the storms of life, I am calm, cool, and collected because my mind is focused on Jesus. He keeps me in perfect peace. I have confidence in God's Word, and I trust Him to bring it to pass. I am assured that He will never leave me or forsake me.

I cast all my cares on Him; in obedience to God's Word, I choose not to worry or be anxious about anything. I will not allow myself to be fearful and troubled about any circumstance in my life. Health and healing are mine. Jesus paid the price for them and His Word says they're mine. I have released my faith, I have received my healing according to the promise of His Word, and now all that is left for me to do is rest in Him until the complete manifestation of healing comes to pass.

My God has promised to give His beloved sweet sleep. Therefore, I receive a full night's sleep every night, and I fully expect to wake up in the morning refreshed, revitalized, and raring to go.

Scripture Confessions

Thou wilt keep him in perfect peace, whose mind is stayed on thee: because he trusteth in thee.

ISAIAH 26:3

(The LORD thy God is a merciful God;) he will not forsake thee.

DEUTERONOMY 4:31

When thou liest down, thou shalt not be afraid: yea, thou shalt lie down, and thy sleep shall be sweet.

PROVERBS 3:24

[The Lord said] I will never leave thee, nor forsake thee.

HEBREWS 13:5

Personal Confessions

SCRIPTURE CONFESSIONS FOR FINANCES

START THE DAY WITH GOD FOR FINANCES

This is the day that the Lord has made, and I will rejoice and be glad in it. My God supplies all my needs according to His riches in glory. It is His will that I prosper and lack nothing. I am the head and not the tail. I am above and not beneath. I am blessed coming in and I am blessed going out. I am blessed on my job; I have God's favor with all those who are in authority over me.

Abraham's blessing is mine. Abundance and prosperity are God's will for my life. I call all of my debts "paid off" and all of my bills "paid on time." Whatever I do succeeds, and I prosper in whatever I put my hand to. I operate and function in the wisdom of God concerning all my financial matters. Men give to me good measure, pressed down and shaken together, and running over. Supernatural money-making ideas come to me. God gives me supernatural insight and understanding on how to make more money and how to manage all of my financial affairs. I have more than enough to meet all of my needs and plenty left over to be a blessing to others.

Scripture Confessions

The LORD shall make thee the head, and not the tail; and thou shalt be above only, and thou shalt not be beneath.

DEUTERONOMY 28:13

The LORD shall preserve thy going out and thy coming in from this time forth, and even for evermore.

PSALM 121:8

Give, and it shall be given unto you; good measure, pressed down, and shaken together, and running over, shall men give into your bosom. For with the same measure that ye mete withal it shall be measured to you again.

LUKE 6:38

GOD IS MY SOURCE

My God supplies all my needs according to His riches in glory. It is God's will that I prosper. He is Jehovah-Jireh, my provider. Jesus was made poor that I might become rich. I am blessed by the Lord, and if I honor Him, He will honor me. Wealth and riches are in my house. The Lord is my shepherd; He takes care of me. Therefore, I shall not suffer from want or lack anything. I do not fear, I am not troubled or anxious, and I do not worry about my finances.

I know that God takes care of the birds and the flowers, and I am much more important to Him than they are. And since I know that He takes care of them, then for sure I know He will take good care of me. Therefore, I will not worry about where I will get the money I need for the necessities of life such as food, rent, car payments, clothes, or mortgage payments. My job is not my source, my relatives are not my source, and my credit cards are not my source. God is my source of supply, and He will never let me down.

Scripture Confessions

My God shall supply all your need according to his riches in glory by Christ Jesus.

Philippians 4:19

Ye know the grace of our Lord Jesus Christ, that, though he was rich, yet for your sakes he became poor, that ye through his poverty might be rich.

2 Corinthians 8:9

Even the very hairs of your head are all numbered. Fear not therefore: ye are of more value than many sparrows.

Luke 12:7

Humility and the fear of the LORD bring wealth and honor and life.

Proverbs 22:4 NIV

THE TITHE

I am a tither! The tithe is the Lord's, and it is a privilege and honor to give Him 10 percent of all my income. When I am obedient to do so, then the windows of heaven are opened to me and they pour out overwhelming blessings of abundance. Because I am a tither, God has promised to rebuke the devourer for my sake. Therefore, the devourer is rebuked in my life. My possessions don't wear out as quickly as they used to. They last much longer than their normal life expectancy. Even my vehicles last longer and run better, and my household appliances work better and longer than normal. Satan's strategies to steal, hinder, or stop my financial blessings are rendered null and void.

As I give my tithe, I honor the Lord and declare that my financial prosperity is independent of the world's system. No matter what the economy does, my finances are blessed. No matter what the stock market does, my finances are blessed. No matter what the interest rates are, my finances are blessed. No matter what the price of gas, God will supply all of my needs. Because I am faithful to honor God, He will honor me. He is faithful to bring abundance and prosperity to me.

Scripture Confessions

Then Jacob made a vow, saying, "If God will be with me, and keep me in this way that I am going, and give me bread to eat and clothing to put on, so that I come back to my father's house in peace, then the LORD shall be my God. And this stone which I have set as a pillar shall be God's house, and of all that You give me I will surely give a tenth to You."

GENESIS 28:20-22 NKJV

Bring ye all the tithes into the storehouse, that there may be meat in mine house, and prove me now herewith, saith the LORD of hosts, if I will not open you the windows of heaven, and pour you out a blessing, that there shall not be room enough to receive it. And I will rebuke the devourer for your sakes.

MALACHI 3:10-11

I give tithes of all that I possess.

LUKE 18:12

My God shall supply all your need according to his riches in glory by Christ Jesus.

PHILIPPIANS 4:19

BEING LED BY THE HOLY SPIRIT IN YOUR FINANCES

Jesus sent the Holy Spirit to be my counselor, guide, and partner in all areas of my life. Therefore, I acknowledge Him and receive Him as my financial advisor. He leads, guides, and directs me in every financial decision of my life. I am led by the Holy Spirit in all financial matters. I am keen to hear and quick to obey the Holy Spirit in all areas concerning my finances. I am sensitive to His voice because I walk in the Spirit. I will not fulfill the lust of my flesh by buying things I don't need, and I won't spend money on foolish pursuits.

I will not enter into any financial arrangement or transaction until I have the peace of God in my spirit regarding what I should do. I will not let my flesh or another person pressure me into buying something that I don't have peace about. Whenever I have a financial decision to make, the Holy Spirit gives me clear and distinct direction. The Lord has given me wisdom, insight, and discernment concerning every detail of my financial affairs.

Scripture Confessions

As many are led by the Spirit of God, they are the sons of God.

ROMANS 8:14

Sojourn in this land, and I will be with thee, and will bless thee; for unto thee, and unto thy seed, I will give all these countries, and I will perform the oath which I sware unto Abraham thy father; And I will make thy seed to multiply as the stars of heaven, and will give unto thy seed all these countries; and in thy seed shall all the nations of the earth be blessed.

GENESIS 26:3-4

Blessed is the man that walketh not in the counsel of the ungodly, nor standeth in the way of sinners, nor sitteth in the seat of the scornful. But his delight is in the law of the LORD; and in his law doth he meditate day and night. And he shall be like a tree planted by the rivers of water, that bringeth forth his fruit in his season; his leaf also shall not wither; and whatsoever he doeth shall prosper.

PSALM 1:1-3

Receive my instruction, and not silver; and knowledge rather than choice gold. For wisdom is better than rubies; and all the things that may be desired are not to be compared to it. I wisdom dwell with prudence, and find out knowledge of witty inventions.

PROVERBS 8:10-12

STRESS-FREE LIVING

I resist stress in my life. I know that it is not God's will for me to be frustrated or fearful about anything. Therefore, I cast all my cares, all my anxieties, all my worry, and all stress over on God. The power of the Holy Spirit in me is greater than any stress that tries to come into my life. I receive God's peace in exchange.

I will not let circumstances and the frustration of daily living bring stress into my life. I will not allow stress to infiltrate my mind.

God promised in His Word that He would give me joy in the middle of problems, tests, and trials. I thank God for that joy and peace in my life. No matter what challenges I might face, I will not become stressed. No matter how burdensome and difficult the problems become, I will not become stressed. I will not allow stress to steal my joy.

Because my trust is in God, I boldly proclaim that stress has no part in me. I choose to walk peaceably, calmly, and confidently before God, knowing that God will provide all that I need. Through my union with Him and the power of the Holy Spirit working in me, I can live a stress-free life.

Scripture Confessions

Casting all your care upon him; for he careth for you.
1 PETER 5:7

Do not be anxious about anything, but in everything, by prayer and petition, with thanksgiving, present your requests to God.

PHILIPPIANS 4:6 NIV

And the peace of God, which transcends all understanding, will guard your hearts and your minds in Christ Jesus.

PHILIPPIANS 4:7 NIV

CONTROLLING MY SPENDING HABITS

I walk in the Spirit; therefore, I will not fulfill the lust of my flesh. I will not let the temptation of jealousy, pride, or envy influence my spending decisions. I am a faithful steward over the money that comes to me. I will not give in to the temptation to lust after material things, as things are not my God. I don't care what people think; I am free from the peer pressure of other people. I am in control of my emotions and of my flesh. I will not go into debt for trivial things. I will not charge items on credit cards unless I know that I can pay for them by the end of the month. I am in total and complete control of my spending.

I will not allow my flesh or pressure from others to force me into compromising my decision to be a good steward over my finances. It's easy for me to say no to poor financial decisions. God has promised that if I will seek Him first, then all the things that I need will be added to me. It is easy for me to be patient and steadfast in my faith until I see the manifestation of the things I really need.

Scripture Confessions

Walk in the Spirit, and ye shall not fulfil the lust of the flesh.

GALATIANS 5:16

Take no thought, saying, What shall we eat? or What shall we drink? or, Wherewithal shall we be clothed? ...But seek ye first the kingdom of God, and his righteousness; and all these things shall be added unto you.

MATTHEW 6:31,33

The simple believes every word, But the prudent considers well his steps.

PROVERBS 14:15 NKJV

Teach me knowledge and good judgment, for I believe in your commands.

PSALM 119:66 NIV

GOD'S MERCY

God is good and His mercy endures forever. He is faithful and just to forgive me of my sins and help me to stay on track. God is a good God, and it is His will for me to prosper and to enjoy good things. God is not mad at me; He loves me and He wants to bless me with abundance. No matter how many times I have messed up—even if what I did was really bad—He still loves me. He doesn't condemn me, and He's not disappointed in me. He is cheering me on because He wants me to succeed.

Even when I make stupid mistakes, God still loves me. Even when I fail Him, He still loves me. Even when I miss the mark and slide into sin, He still loves me and is quick to forgive me when I confess my sins. Even when my financial difficulties are the result of my own poor decisions, He still promises to deliver me, restore me, and prosper me. His plan for my life is success and abundance. He will never fail me even when I fail Him. He crowns my life with tender mercies and lovingkindness.

Scripture Confessions

If we confess our sins, he is faithful and just to forgive us our sins, and to cleanse us from all unrighteousness.

1 John 1:9

If my people, which are called by my name, shall humble themselves, and pray, and seek my face, and turn from their wicked ways; then will I hear from heaven, and will forgive their sin, and will heal their land.

2 Chronicles 7:14

Remember, O LORD, thy tender mercies and thy lovingkindness; for they have been ever of old.

Psalm 25:6

For You, Lord, are good, and ready to forgive, And abundant in mercy to all those who call upon You.

Psalm 86:5 NKJV

GOD'S BLESSINGS AT WORK

I am faithful and diligent to do my job with excellence. I will do my best to honor God by giving my employer my best, and they will be glad they hired me. I will perform my daily tasks at work with a great attitude, with impeccable integrity, and as a workman worthy of his hire.

Because I am faithful, I will abound in blessings. God gives me insight and understanding on how to do my job better. He shows me ways to perform my duties in an exceptional manner and how to work more effectively and efficiently. Because God's favor is on me and I do my job with excellence, I believe my employer will recognize my value and contribution to the organization and will give me raises, bonuses, and promotions as a result. God prospers the company I work for so they can bless me.

God gives me new and creative ideas on how to make money. I do my work as unto the Lord. Whatever I put my hand to prospers. Because I am faithful in what is another man's, and because I am faithful over little things, the Lord will see to it that I am promoted to bigger things.

Scripture Confessions

The labourer is worthy of his hire.

LUKE 10:7

Blessings shall come on thee, and overtake thee, if thou shalt hearken unto the voice of the LORD thy God.

DEUTERONOMY 28:2

Keep the charge of the LORD thy God, to walk in his ways, to keep his statutes, and his commandments, and his judgments, and his testimonies, as it is written in the law of Moses, that thou mayest prosper in all that thou doest and whithersoever thou turnest thyself.

1 KINGS 2:3

Well done, good and faithful servant; thou has been faithful over a few things, I will make thee ruler over many things.

MATTHEW 25:23

Prioritizing My Time

I am in control of my day. I choose to redeem my time, focus my attention on my priorities, and have a super productive day. I refuse to get sidetracked, distracted, or diverted from my priorities. I will work diligently, think clearly, and perform my duties with excellence. I will not waste my time by procrastinating, poor planning, or being lazy. I have all the energy I need to get my work done. I am effective and efficient in all that I do.

The Holy Spirit in me shows me how to work smarter and helps me avoid obstacles before they become apparent. I am not easily distracted, and I remain focused and on target concerning the task at hand. I have a spirit of excellence and do all my duties to the very best of my ability. I am organized, disciplined, and focused. I finish what I start, and I am constantly finding better ways to make my day more productive.

I have a great attitude and a steady spirit. I am not easily frustrated or flustered by unexpected events. I respond with calmness and confidence to any problem or challenge that may present itself. God in me is greater than anything I might face today.

Scripture Confessions

But his delight is in the law of the LORD; and in his law doth he meditate day and night.

PSALM 1:2

He becometh poor that dealeth with a slack hand: but the hand of the diligent maketh rich.

PROVERBS 10:4

Walk in wisdom toward them that are without, redeeming the time.

COLOSSIANS 4:5

Ye are of God, little children, and have overcome them: because greater is he that is in you, than he that is in the world.

1 JOHN 4:4

WHEN BAD NEWS COMES ABOUT YOUR FINANCES

I am not shaken when I hear bad news. I will not let a bad report affect my joy or rob me of my peace. I will not let bad news discourage me or cause me to become fearful. God has a plan for me to overcome this financial adversity. This was no surprise to Him. He will make a way where there seems to be no way. I cast all the problems of this situation over on the Lord. I will not let worry, fear, or anxious thoughts trouble me. The Holy Spirit gives me insight, wisdom, and favor to navigate my way through this adversity.

God is my provider, deliverer, and strong tower. I have learned to live independent of circumstances. The Holy Spirit gives me clear and specific directions concerning what I should do. Jesus will never leave me nor forsake me. Therefore I will not let my heart be troubled. I will trust in God and I will boast in His Word. What the enemy has meant for evil, God will turn it to my good. I will patiently wait and see the salvation of the Lord.

Scripture Confessions

I will even make a way in the wilderness.

ISAIAH 43:19

Let not your heart be troubled; ye believe in God, believe also in me.

JOHN 14:1

Let not your heart be troubled, neither let it be afraid.

JOHN 14:27

[The Lord said] I will never leave thee, nor forsake thee.

HEBREWS 13:5

FEAR CONCERNING YOUR FINANCES

I will not allow fear to get a grip on my life. I trust the Lord and believe His Word instead of letting fear control my thoughts or actions. I have the peace of God, which transcends all understanding and guards my heart and my mind. God is on my side. He is working on my behalf. He will deliver me, He will sustain me, and He will give me peace no matter what the circumstances. God has not given me a spirit of fear, but of power, love, and a sound mind. My confidence is in the Lord, whose Word is greater than the voice of fear trying to invade my mind.

The God of Abraham, Isaac, and Jacob—the wondrous God who brought His people out of the land of Egypt with a mighty hand—will preserve me and protect me. I am not worried or fearful about anything. God is working all things out in my life for my good. I will not make decisions, initiate any conversation, or give any advice based on fear. I have authority in the name of Jesus. God's love sustains me and comforts me. I will not allow fear to influence any part of my life. I resist the attacks of the enemy who would try to bring fear into my life.

Scripture Confessions

The peace of God, which transcends all understanding, will guard your hearts and your minds in Christ Jesus.

PHILIPPIANS 4:7 NIV

You did not receive a spirit that makes you a slave again to fear, but you received the Spirit of sonship. And by him we cry, "Abba, Father."

ROMANS 8:15 NIV

SPEAK TO THE MOUNTAIN OF DEBT

Jesus said that if I speak to the mountain in my life it will have to obey me. Therefore, I speak to the mountain of debt in my life and command it to be gone. No matter how big the mountain of debt is, it's not bigger than my God.

I speak to all my debt, and I command it to be paid. Debts, I'm talking to you and telling you to be paid in Jesus' name. Debts, be reduced and eliminated. I call my mortgage paid in Jesus' name. I call my vehicles paid off in Jesus' name. I call every loan and credit card paid off in Jesus' name. My God can bring water out of a rock, and He can feed thousands with a few pieces of fish and bread. My God can surely take care of my bills.

I declare that my God meets all my needs; therefore, all my bills are paid on time. I refuse to worry or have any anxious thought about my finances. I don't have to figure out where the money is coming from because that's God's concern. I have released my faith. Now I shall receive my provision.

Scripture Confessions

If ye have faith as a grain of mustard seed, ye shall say unto this mountain, Remove hence to yonder place; and it shall remove; and nothing shall be impossible unto you.

MATTHEW 17:20

They thirsted not when he led them through the deserts: he caused the waters to flow out of the rock for them: he clave the rock also, and the waters gushed out.

ISAIAH 48:21

Jesus went forth, and saw a great multitude, and was moved with compassion toward them, and he healed their sick. And when it was evening, his disciples came to him, saying, This is a desert place, and the time is now past; send the multitude away, that they may go into the villages, and buy themselves victuals. But Jesus said unto them, They need not depart; give ye them to eat. And they say unto him, We have here but five loaves, and two fishes. He said, Bring them hither to me. And he commanded the multitude to sit down on the grass, and took the five loaves, and the two fishes, and looking up to heaven, he blessed, and brake, and gave the loaves to his disciples, and the disciples to the multitude.

MATTHEW 14:14-19

But my God shall supply all your need according to his riches in glory by Christ Jesus.

PHILIPPIANS 4:19

END THE DAY WITH GOD FOR FINANCES

The peace of God places garrisons around me. His peace gives me strength, comfort, and rest from all the events, circumstances, and challenges of this life. I will not carry the burden of my financial difficulties. Instead, I will cast all my care on Him. I will not worry or be anxious about anything. I will not let my mind or heart become troubled. Jesus will never leave me or forsake me. No weapon formed against me shall prosper. If God be for me, then surely no one can be against me.

God is working on my behalf. All of my debts are being eliminated and paid off. All my bills are paid on time. If my income is not enough to cover all my expenses, then God will make up the difference. God has promised to give His beloved sweet sleep, and I am His beloved, so that means me. I will sleep soundly and peacefully throughout the whole night. I will wake refreshed and encouraged and full of joy, ready to face a new day.

Scripture Confessions

God's peace [shall be yours, that tranquil state of a soul assured of its salvation through Christ, and so fearing nothing from God and being content with its earthly lot of whatever sort that is, that peace] which transcends all understanding shall garrison mount guard over your hearts and minds in Christ Jesus.

PHILIPPIANS 4:7 AMP

No weapon that is formed against thee shall prosper.

ISAIAH 54:17

Peace I leave with you, my peace I give unto you; not as the world giveth, give I unto you. Let not your heart be troubled, neither let it be afraid.

JOHN 14:27

When thou liest down, thou shalt not be afraid: yea, thou shalt lie down, and thy sleep shall be sweet.

PROVERBS 3:24

Personal Confessions

SCRIPTURE
CONFESSIONS
FOR PARENTING

START THE DAY WITH
GOD FOR PARENTS

This is the day the Lord has made, and I will rejoice and be glad in it. God's mercy and grace are new every morning in the lives of my children.

My children are a wonderful gift and blessing from God. I believe they will always bring me great joy and not heartache. They are the blessed of the Lord, and today will be a great day for them—a day of joy, peace, and fulfillment. God's Word will guide their steps, and God's peace will protect their hearts. They are strong in the Lord and the power of His might.

God's favor surrounds them like a shield; they will be sensitive to the Holy Spirit today and be quick to recognize and obey His voice. The Holy Spirit will give them wisdom and discernment regarding every decision they need to make today.

Wherever they go and whatever they do, they will be protected from harm, evil, and danger of any kind.

My children will be carriers of God's love and joy. They are a shining light in a world of darkness. They are quick to reach out to others in need. They are bold in their faith and strong in their convictions. They will not give in to peer pressure to do wrong things; instead, their faith and courage will be strength to their friends.

Scripture Confessions

It is of the LORD's mercies that we are not consumed, because his compassions fail not. They are new every morning: great is thy faithfulness.

LAMENTATIONS 3:22,23

In all thy ways acknowledge him, and he shall direct thy paths.

PROVERBS 3:6

Let no corrupt communication proceed out of your mouth, but that which is good to the use of edifying, that it may minister grace unto the hearers.

EPHESIANS 4:29

I can do all things through Christ which strengtheneth me.

PHILIPPIANS 4:13

What shall we then say to these things? If God be for us, who can be against us?

ROMANS 8:31

BECOMING THE PARENT GOD SAYS I AM

I choose to glorify God in my role as a parent. I choose to live a godly life before my children. I am disciplined concerning my priorities, and I manage my time in an effective and efficient manner. I am sensitive to the needs of my children. I have God's wisdom and discernment concerning how all my decisions affect their lives.

I am loving, caring, and compassionate toward my children. I keep my cool during times of stress and do not become frustrated and lose my temper. If I do something that is wrong or offensive, I am quick to repent and make things right. Because I live a Spirit-controlled life, I am peaceful, consistent, and faithful. I walk in love at all times, and I am quick to provide encouragement and inspiration to my family. I refuse to criticize, condemn, or complain to or about my kids. I will be honest and truthful and live my life with integrity. When faced with the need to discipline my children, I will do so without anger. I will reference God's Word as their standard of conduct.

I will be steadfast and resolute regarding my convictions and will do my best to model the life of a godly parent before my kids. I will be faithful to pray for my children. With the help of the Holy Spirit, I will do my best to mentor and instruct them in the truth and principles of God's Word.

Scripture Confessions

...we should live soberly, righteously, and godly, in this present world.

TITUS 2:12

If any of you lack wisdom, let him ask of God, that giveth to all men liberally, and upbraideth not; and it shall be given him.

JAMES 1:5

...be thou an example of the believers, in word, in conversation, in charity, in spirit, in faith, in purity.

1 TIMOTHY 4:12

GODLY HOUSEHOLD

My home is a place of refuge and peace. I believe that anyone who comes into my home will feel the presence of God. I choose to honor God in my home. I dedicate my home to the Lord; I consecrate it with prayer and praise.

I am diligent and committed to monitor and evaluate the kinds of books, videos, music, and movies that are allowed to be played in my home.

In my home are riches and honor; my God supplies all my family's needs. I will work diligently to keep my house clean and beautiful so that it is a constant blessing to all my family.

I believe my home is a safe haven, protected and kept safe by God's divine protection. I believe no evil shall come near my home, and no plague, disease, or calamity shall befall us. I believe my home is blessed and all who enter it are blessed.

My home is consecrated and dedicated to God. I will not allow activities in my home that are not honorable to God. With the Holy Spirit's help I will create and maintain an atmosphere of love, hope, and peace in my home. I believe everyone who comes to my home will sense His presence.

Scripture Confessions

...as for me and my house, we will serve the LORD.

JOSHUA 24:15

And they shall teach my people the difference between the holy and profane, and cause them to discern between the unclean and the clean.

EZEKIEL 44:23

And now abideth faith, hope, charity, these three; but the greatest of these is charity.

1 CORINTHIANS 13:13

But my God shall supply all your need according to his riches in glory by Christ Jesus.

PHILIPPIANS 4:19

There shall no evil befall thee, neither shall any plague come nigh thy dwelling.

PSALM 91:10

THE GREATER ONE IN MY CHILDREN

God Himself makes His home in the hearts of my children. God in them is greater than any temptation, greater than any peer pressure, greater than any sin, greater than Satan and all the forces of darkness. God in my children is greater than any problem or obstacle they might face, greater than sickness or disease, greater than sin or any challenge that comes in their lives.

He is greater than any adversity they might face. He is greater than their doubts, insecurities, or uncertainties. He is greater than fear, worry, or anxiety.

The Spirit of God lives in them. He helps them to succeed, He puts them over, and He causes them to be victorious in their everyday lives.

God's Word gives them boldness and courage to live godly lives before their family and friends. The same Spirit that raised Christ Jesus from the dead lives in my children. The Holy Spirit quickens and brings life, strength, and vitality to their bodies. My children are more than conquerors in Christ Jesus through the power of the Holy Spirit. My children shall face life with confidence and a resolute, tenacious faith in God, who always causes them to triumph in life. Greater is He that is in them than he that is in the world.

Ye are of God, little children, and have overcome them: because greater is he that is in you, than he that is in the world.

1 JOHN 4:4

These things I have spoken unto you, that in me ye might have peace. In the world ye shall have tribulation: but be of good cheer; I have overcome the world.

JOHN 16:33

Nay, in all these things we are more than conquerors through him that loved us.

ROMANS 8:37

But if the Spirit of him that raised up Jesus from the dead dwell in you, he that raised up Christ from the dead shall also quicken your mortal bodies by his Spirit that dwelleth in you.

ROMANS 8:11

MY CHILDREN'S
SPIRITUAL GROWTH

I speak God's Word over my children. I proclaim and confess that my children are strong in faith. God's Word is working in their lives. They have pure hearts, and they conduct their lives with honesty, purity, and integrity. They love God's Word and desire to live honorable lives before Him. Favor surrounds them like a shield. They are sensitive to the Holy Spirit, and they are quick to obey His voice. They are bold in their faith and want to share it with others.

My children are growing strong spiritually, mentally, and physically. They have wisdom functioning in every area of their lives. They put God's Word first and accept it as final authority in their lives. They are careful what influences they allow in their lives. The eyes of their understanding are opened to the truth of God's Word.

They have godly discernment concerning the type of people they develop relationships with. They are not easily fooled or deceived and have godly wisdom beyond their years.

They are individuals of character and principle. They are kind, loving, and giving towards others. They are not selfish or self-serving. They are quick to reach out to help others in need. They will develop into courageous, confident, and determined adults, ready to fulfill the plans that God has for them.

Scripture Confessions

He restoreth my soul: he leadeth me in the paths of righteousness for his name's sake.

PSALM 23:3

But the Comforter, which is the Holy Ghost, whom the Father will send in my name, he shall teach you all things, and bring all things to your remembrance, whatsoever I have said unto you.

JOHN 14:26

For I know the thoughts that I think toward you, saith the LORD, thoughts of peace, and not of evil, to give you an expected end.

JEREMIAH 29:11

MY CHILDREN HEAR GOD'S VOICE

I proclaim that my children know God's voice and will not be deceived by the voice of the enemy. They are sensitive to the voice of the Holy Spirit and are quick to obey His instruction, direction, and guidance. They are tuned in to the Holy Spirit and quickly recognize His voice. They are mindful not to do anything that grieves the Holy Spirit. They are diligent to spend time in prayer, to fellowship, and to worship the Lord so that they continually keep themselves in proper spiritual condition to hear His voice.

My children will seek God's wisdom and counsel concerning all matters of their lives. I know He will be faithful to speak to them concerning changes or corrections they need to make. I believe they will be faithful to do everything God would have them to do. He speaks to my children through His Word. As they study and meditate on the Scriptures, God's lifegiving force comes alive in their hearts. God's Word enlightens their spirits and illuminates their minds. I believe that my children's union with God grows stronger every day, as well as their ability to hear His voice clearly and accurately.

Scripture Confessions

But this thing commanded I them, saying, Obey my voice, and I will be your God, and ye shall be my people: and walk ye in all the ways that I have commanded you, that it may be well unto you.

JEREMIAH 7:23

And when he putteth forth his own sheep, he goeth before them, and the sheep follow him: for they know his voice. And a stranger will they not follow, but will flee from him: for they know not the voice of strangers.

JOHN 10:4-5

My sheep hear my voice, and I know them, and they follow me.

JOHN 10:27

So then faith cometh by hearing, and hearing by the word of God.

ROMANS 10:17

GOD'S WISDOM FOR MY CHILDREN

God's Word says that Jesus has been made unto us wisdom. God's wisdom is flowing in my children, providing guidance, insight, and discernment in every area of their lives.

God's wisdom in them gives them foresight and understanding concerning all issues in their lives. God's wisdom teaches them to properly manage their time and prioritize their activities.

I believe my children have wisdom beyond their years. They are level-headed and are able to think clearly and accurately when faced with perplexing situations. Because of God's wisdom in my children's lives, they will make wise choices concerning their friends. They will be able to discern the consequences of their choices; therefore, it will be easy for them to make wise decisions.

They have a sense of what is right and wrong. They are learning how to let God's wisdom be perfected in their lives. They are wise counselors and are able to have a positive impact on their family and friends.

Because my children walk in the wisdom of God, they make significant and meaningful contributions to the lives of others. The lies and deceptions of the enemy do not fool my children. They recognize and reject any course of action that would possibly lead them in the wrong direction.

My children are goal-oriented and understand that the consequences of their choices today are the building blocks of their future.

Scripture Confessions

If any of you lack wisdom, let him ask of God, that giveth to all men liberally, and upbraideth not; and it shall be given him.

JAMES 1:5

The steps of a good man are ordered by the LORD: and he delighteth in his way.

PSALM 37:23

Through wisdom is an house builded; and by understanding it is established.

PROVERBS 24:3

FAVOR FOR MY CHILDREN

My children are blessed and highly favored. The favor of God is operating and functioning daily in their lives. It surrounds them like a shield. The favor of God goes before them and prepares their way. Favor opens doors of blessing and opportunity in every area of their lives. Wherever they go and whatever they do, God's favor is with them and on them.

God's favor is operating and functioning in every area of their lives. They have favor with family and in all of their relationships. They have favor at school with friends and with teachers. They have favor with their coaches and team members. They have favor at church and with other kids.

All their endeavors are blessed, because God's blessings of favor come to them every day. Whatever they set their hands to prospers and succeeds because of His favor. God's favor brings promotion and increase in their lives. God's favor fills their lives with overflowing blessings of peace, joy, fulfillment, and abundance.

Scripture Confessions

When a man's ways please the LORD, he maketh even his enemies to be at peace with him.

PROVERBS 16:7

For thou, LORD, wilt bless the righteous; with favour wilt thou compass him as with a shield.

PSALM 5:12

I know thy works: behold, I have set before thee an open door, and no man can shut it....

REVELATION 3:8

My Children Are Obedient to Authority

My children are obedient to me, and they are quick to respond to my requests. They honor me and respect me. They are kind and considerate and are quick to repent if they ever do anything to offend me.

Because they respect me, they do not ignore me when I speak to them but give me their undivided attention. They are not slothful in fulfilling their chores and household duties.

As my children honor me, so will I honor them and respect them. I will never belittle or talk to them in a condescending way. I will always be looking for opportunities to tell and show them how much I love them. God will bless and honor them because they honor those who are in authority over their lives.

They will not give in to the temptation to be prideful or rebellious. The truth of God's Word that has been planted in their hearts is the guiding light of their lives. They have God's nature in their hearts and a pleasant disposition.

Because they are obedient to me, they shall have blessed lives, and they shall live long and fruitful lives.

Scripture Confessions

Children, obey your parents in the Lord: for this is right. Honor thy father and mother; which is the first commandment with promise; That it may be well with thee, and thou mayest live long on the earth.

Ephesians 6:1-3

For kings, and for all that are in authority; that we may lead a quiet and peaceable life in all godliness and honesty.

1 Timothy 2:2

And the people said unto Joshua, The LORD our God will we serve, and his voice will we obey.

Joshua 24:24

If ye be willing and obedient, ye shall eat the good of the land.

Isaiah 1:19

MY CHILDREN ARE BOLD AND COURAGEOUS

My children are bold and courageous. They are quick to stand up for truth and right. They do not have a spirit of timidity or fear. They are strong in the Lord and the power of His might. The Holy Spirit lives big and bold in my children. Fear will not intimidate my children. Anxiety or worry will not control them. Peer pressure will not push them. My children are steadfast in their convictions. When faced with the temptation to compromise, they will make the right choice.

They are confident in God and in themselves, knowing that greater is He that is in them than he that is in the world. They recognize the devil for who he is, a defeated foe, a loser, and a weak, humiliated enemy of God. The devil is no match for my children because they serve the Lord and are filled with the Spirit of the Most High God.

They will not cower or waver in times of adversity, but will face challenges with courage and the heart of a warrior. They are more than conquerors through Jesus Christ.

My children can do all things through Christ who gives them strength, knowledge, and wisdom to overcome any obstacle.

Scripture Confessions

Ye are of God, little children, and have overcome them: because greater is he that is in you, than he that is in the world.

1 JOHN 4:4

Nay, in all these things we are more than conquerors through him that loved us.

ROMANS 8:37

For whatsoever is born of God overcometh the world: and this is the victory that overcometh the world, even our faith.

1 JOHN 5:4

DIVINE PROTECTION FOR MY FAMILY

God's Word promises divine protection for the children of God. Therefore, I proclaim that no evil shall come near me or my family. No plague shall come near us; though a thousand may fall at our side and ten thousand at our right hand, it shall not, will not, cannot come near my family.

God's angels encamp around us. The angels of the Lord have charge over us to protect and keep us from danger, harm, and injury of any kind.

Though we walk through the fire we will not be burned. If we find ourselves in flood waters, they will not overtake us. Though we walk through the valley of the shadow of death, we will fear no evil, for God is with us. No weapon formed against my family shall prosper.

God is our refuge and fortress. He will deliver us from the traps of the enemy, and He will deliver us from deadly diseases. Under God's wings we take refuge, and His truth is our shield and protection from all the dangers of this world. I plead the blood of Jesus over my family, over any vehicle we ride in, over the schools, and over any house or building we go into.

We shall not fall prey to the schemes and traps of Satan. We walk with wisdom and discernment and quickly heed God's voice. My family shall live long on the earth. We will fulfill the plans and purposes God has designed for us.

Scripture Confessions

Let your conversation be without covetousness; and be content with such things as ye have: for he hath said, I will never leave thee, nor forsake thee.

HEBREWS 13:5

Keep me as the apple of the eye, hide me under the shadow of thy wings.

PSALM 17:8

There shall no evil befall thee, neither shall any plague come nigh thy dwelling.

PSALM 91:10

And the peace of God, which passeth all understanding, shall keep your hearts and minds through Christ Jesus.

PHILIPPIANS 4:7

HEALTH AND HEALING FOR MY CHILDREN

I proclaim healing over my children. By Jesus' stripes they were healed. The healing, life-giving, disease-destroying power of God is working in their bodies. It drives out all manner of sickness and disease. They are full of life, health, strength, and vitality. They are healed, healthy, and whole from the tops of their heads to the soles of their feet. Every organ in their bodies operates and functions the way God created it, with no disease or malfunctions. Every system in their bodies operates and functions with supernatural efficiency. My children's nervous systems, their lymphatic systems, their digestive systems, their electrical systems, their circulatory systems, and every other system function with 100 percent efficiency.

Jesus Himself bore my children's sicknesses and carried their diseases; therefore, sickness and disease are not allowed to exist in their bodies. Their bodies are free from growths, tumors, or obstructions of any kind.

The divine zoe-life of God flows through them, quickening and making alive their mortal bodies. My children's bodies are free from pain, discomfort, distress, and all symptoms of sickness. God's Word is medicine to their flesh. I am not moved by how they feel, how they look, or any negative reports, because I believe God's Word and His Word says they are healed. My children are healed, healthy, and whole in Jesus' name.

Scripture Confessions

But he was wounded for our transgressions, he was bruised for our iniquities: the chastisement of our peace was upon him; and with his stripes we are healed.

ISAIAH 53:5

My son, attend to my words; incline thine ear unto my sayings. Let them not depart from thine eyes; keep them in the midst of thine heart. For they are life unto those that find them, and health to all their flesh.

PROVERBS 4:20-22

He sent his word, and healed them, and delivered them from their destructions.

PSALM 107:20

That it might be fulfilled which was spoken by Esaias the prophet, saying, Himself took our infirmities, and bare our sicknesses.

MATTHEW 8:17

Who his own self bare our sins in his own body on the tree, that we, being dead to sins, should live unto righteousness: by whose stripes ye were healed.

1 PETER 2:24

FOR MY CHILDREN TO LIVE A HEALTHY LIFESTYLE

I believe my children will make healthy lifestyle choices regarding what they eat and drink.

God's Word says our body is the temple of the Holy Spirit. I believe that my children are good stewards of their bodies. They choose to walk in the Spirit; therefore, they do not fulfill the lusts of their flesh. They are strong in their convictions and will have the strength to say no to any action that could cause potential harm to their bodies.

They choose to eat and drink only what is good for them, and they will not abuse their bodies by eating or drinking things that are harmful and destructive to them.

My children recognize the value of developing a daily regiment of physical exercise that keeps their bodies trim and fit, operating at their optimum. They get plenty of sleep so their bodies are able to renew themselves daily.

My children make healthy lifestyle choices and reap the benefits of a healthy body.

Scripture Confessions

What? know ye not that your body is the temple of the Holy Ghost which is in you, which ye have of God, and ye are not your own?

1 CORINTHIANS 6:19

I beseech you therefore, brethren, by the mercies of God, that ye present your bodies a living sacrifice, holy, acceptable unto God, which is your reasonable service.

ROMANS 12:1

This I say then, Walk in the Spirit, and ye shall not fulfill the lust of the flesh.

GALATIANS 5:16

MY CHILDREN'S SELF-IMAGE

My children have a healthy self-image. They are confident in who they are. They understand that God's love makes them valuable. My children understand that who they are is determined by what God has declared them to be and not by what others say about them. God's Word says that they are precious in His sight. They are children of the Most High God. He has chosen them, and He has great plans for their lives.

My children see themselves as God sees them. They see themselves as more than conquerors through Christ Jesus. They are the head and not the tail, above and not beneath, going over and not under. They see themselves as victorious and triumphant in life.

They are not filled with worry, anxiety, or selfdoubt, but courage, boldness, and faith. They realize that they can do all things though Christ, who strengthens them. They think clearly and rationally.

My children have a positive attitude and will not allow the circumstances of life to steal their peace.

I declare that my children are confident in their relationship with God, and therefore, they are secure in who they are; they do not give in to thoughts and temptations of insecurity.

Scripture Confessions

Ye are of God, little children, and have overcome them: because greater is he that is in you, than he that is in the world.

1 JOHN 4:4

Nay, in all things we are more than conquerors through him that loved us.

ROMANS 8:37

Being confident of this very thing, that he which hath begun a good work in you will perform it until the day of Jesus Christ.

PHILIPPIANS 1:6

I can do all things through Christ which strengtheneth me.

PHILIPPIANS 4:13

FOR MY CHILDREN TO OVERCOME DISCOURAGEMENT

When faced with discouragement, I believe that the Holy Spirit will cause the Word of God that has been sown in my children's hearts to rise up within them. They will respond quickly and with boldness to the temptation to be discouraged or depressed.

Greater is the Spirit of the Lord in them than any problem or challenge they may face. God will put them over; He will give them great success.

My children are more than conquerors through Christ Jesus, who always causes them to triumph over every difficulty or challenge. When faced with bad news or any adversity, they will draw strength from God's Word and the Holy Spirit. My children will not allow the enemy to push or pull them down with anxiety, worry, or depression.

My children are strong in the Lord and the power of His might. They are quick to rejoice and praise God in any circumstance. They draw courage and strength from the Lord to overcome any trial or challenge in their lives.

Scripture Confessions

Many are the afflictions of the righteous: but the LORD delivereth him out of them all.

PSALM 34:19

These things I have spoken unto you, that in me ye might have peace. In the world ye shall have tribulation: but be of good cheer; I have overcome the world.

JOHN 16:33

Then he said unto them, Go your way, eat the fat, and drink the sweet, and send portions unto them for whom nothing is prepared: for this day is holy unto our LORD: neither be ye sorry; for the joy of the LORD is your strength.

NEHEMIAH 8:10

But as for you, ye thought evil against me; but God meant it unto good, to bring to pass, as it is this day, to save much people alive.

GENESIS 50:20

My Children Have Pleasant Personalities

I believe my children are kind and considerate of others. They are eager and willing to be a blessing at any opportunity. They have a heart of compassion, and they are easily touched with the hurt and pain of others. They are quick to speak a kind or encouraging word to a friend who is down or discouraged. They are always willing to lend a helping hand to those in need. They are willing to forego their own pleasures in order to be a blessing to others.

They do their chores without complaining and whining. They are ever ready to do their part in working around the house or in the yard.

They are diligent and responsible regarding their school work and other obligations in their lives. They are respectful of their parents and others in positions of authority in their lives. They do not give in to selfish or self-serving desires but are giving and have a servant's heart.

My children have pleasant and pleasing personalities. They are gracious and mannerly when interacting with others.

Scripture Confessions

But a certain Samaritian, as he journeyed, came where he was: and when he saw him, he had compassion on him, and went to him, and bound up his wounds, pouring in oil and wine, and set him on his own beast, and brought him to an inn, and took care of him.

LUKE 10:33-34

By this shall all men know that ye are my disciples, if ye have love one to another.

JOHN 13:35

A man that hath friends must shew himself friendly: and there is a friend that sticketh closer than a bother.

PROVERBS 18:24

And at the end of ten days their countenances appeared fairer and fatter in flesh than all the children which did eat the portion of the king's meat.

DANIEL 1:15

FOR MY CHILDREN TO CHOOSE GODLY FRIENDS

I know it is God's will for my children to have a godly circle of friends. I believe the Holy Spirit will give them discernment regarding the right kind of friends. I believe God will bring my children godly friends who are strong spiritually, who love God, and who will have a positive impact on my children's lives.

I believe the Holy Spirit will lead my children to friends who love God and have a close relationship with Him. The Holy Spirit will help them to be sensitive to the needs of their friends and to encourage them in their spiritual walk. May God be at the center of all their friendships.

I believe my children will develop strong, healthy friendships that will last a lifetime. I believe my children will recognize the true value of close, godly friends. I believe that my children will come to realize that one of God's greatest gifts in this life is the friendship of a true friend.

Scripture Confessions

If any of you lacks wisdom, he should ask God, who gives generously to all without finding fault, and it will be given to him.

JAMES 1:5 NIV

He that walketh with wise men shall be wise: but a companion of fools shall be destroyed.

PROVERBS 13:20

But speaking the truth in love, may grow up into him in all things, which is the head, even Christ: From whom the whole body fitly joined together and compacted by that which every joint supplieth, according to the effectual working in the measure of every part, maketh increase of the body unto the edifying of itself in love.

EPHESIANS 4:15-16

MY CHILDREN'S FUTURE

God's Word promises me that His covenant blessings are passed down to my children. Therefore, I am in agreement with His Word, and I boldly proclaim that He has prepared a bright and glorious future for my children.

They will live in God's abundance in every area of their lives. God's blessings shall overtake them. They will serve God with gladness and enthusiasm all the days of their lives. My children will honor God by how they conduct their lives. They will be bold witnesses for the kingdom. They have passion and a desire to reach out to hurting people with the good news of the Gospel. They will fulfill all the plans and purposes that God has desired for them to accomplish. God shall direct their steps. They have been trained and nurtured in the Word of God. They will not fall into sin or slide away from God.

God's favor shall be upon them, and they shall succeed at the assignment God has for their lives. My children shall have a spirit of discernment and will not be fooled by people who would try to deceive or discourage them from pursuing God's plan for their lives.

My children will be determined and courageous in their pursuit of all God has for them. They will be quick to take a stand for what is right and against what is wrong. They shall be people of peace and kindness, with a heart of compassion for others.

They will endure hardships as good soldiers and face the obstacles and setbacks of life with courage and spiritual resolve.

My children's lives will be a living testimony of God's love, power, and grace. They will live strong, victorious, God-centered lives.

Scripture Confessions

Being confident of this very thing, that he which hath begun a good work in you will perform it until the day of Jesus Christ.

PHILIPPIANS 1:6

For the gifts and calling of God are without repentance.

ROMANS 11:29

Therefore, since we have such a hope, we are very bold.

2 CORINTHIANS 3:12 NIV

PRAYER OF SALVATION

God loves you—no matter who you are, no matter what your past. God loves you so much that He gave His one and only begotten Son for you. The Bible tells us that "...whoever believes in him shall not perish but have eternal life" (John 3:16 NIV). Jesus laid down His life and rose again so that we could spend eternity with Him in heaven and experience His absolute best on earth. If you would like to receive Jesus into your life, say the following prayer out loud and mean it from your heart.

> *Heavenly Father, I come to You admitting that I am a sinner. Right now, I choose to turn away from sin, and I ask You to cleanse me of all unrighteousness. I believe that Your Son, Jesus, died on the cross to take away my sins. I also believe that He rose again from the dead so that I might be forgiven of my sins and made righteous through faith in Him. I call upon the name of Jesus Christ to be the Savior and Lord of my life. Jesus, I choose to follow You and ask that You fill me with the power of the Holy Spirit. I declare that right now I am a child of God. I am free from sin and full of the righteousness of God. I am saved in Jesus' name. Amen.*

If you prayed this prayer to receive Jesus Christ as your Savior for the first time, please contact us on the Web at www.harrisonhouse.com to receive a free book.

Or you may write to us at

Harrison House

P.O. Box 35035

Tulsa, Oklahoma 74153

Personal Confessions

ABOUT THE AUTHORS

Keith and Megan Provance have been in Christian publishing for over 30 years, with Keith serving as President of Harrison House Publishing for 20 of those years. Together, they founded Word and Spirit Resources, a company dedicated to the publishing and world-wide distribution of life changing books. Keith also works as a publishing consultant to national and international ministries.

Their book, *Pray for Our Nation*, has sold over 1.2 million copies and they have authored several other bestselling books including *Scripture Confessions for Victorious Living, Scripture Confessions for Healing*, and *Scripture Confessions for Finances*. They are the parents of three sons, Ryan, Garrett, and Jacob, and they reside in Tulsa, Oklahoma.

OTHER BOOKS AVAILABLE IN THE SCRIPTURE CONFESSIONS SERIES

Available at bookstores everywhere or visit
www.harrisonhouse.com.

The Harrison House Vision

Proclaiming the truth and the power

of the Gospel of Jesus Christ with excellence.

Challenging Christians

to live victoriously,

grow spiritually,

know God intimately.

Connect with us on

f Facebook @ **HarrisonHousePublishers**

and **◎** Instagram @ **HarrisonHousePublishing**

so you can stay up to date with news

about our books and our authors.

Visit us at **www.harrisonhouse.com**

for a complete product listing as well as

monthly specials for wholesale distribution.